Going Out Without

Freaking Out

Going Out Without Freaking Out

Dating Made Doable

Tim Baker

Kregel
Publications

Going Out Without Freaking Out: Dating Made Doable

© 2004 by Tim Baker

Published by Kregel Publications, P.O. Box 2607, Grand Rapids, MI 49501.

Cover design: John M. Lucas

ISBN   0-8254-2395-3

Printed in the United States of America

04 05 06 07 08 / 5 4 3 2 1

Contents

Acknowledgments

Many thanks to Steve Barclift, Dennis Hillman, and everyone at Kregel Publications. Thanks for your patience and for believing in this project.

Alison Simpson helped greatly with several chapters. Thanks for your research, writing, and creativity.

Julie Zielke, Elizabeth Moss, Laura Johnson, Jenni Summers, Liz Hillman, and numerous other students who looked the initial manuscript over, offered ideas, and gave input—thanks for helping to shape this book.

Jacqui, thanks for giving me time to write this book and for letting people read about our dating experience. I love you!

How to Use This Book

Are you like me? I was a failure at dating. My first flop was a girl who lived three houses down the street. I can't remember her name, and I don't recall what she looked like. But she must have been beautiful. Everything in my seven-year-old body knew that she was the one for me.

Each day I sat on the steps of my house, eating Popsicles and staring at her yard. I daydreamed that she'd come out, notice me, and call for me to come to her. Maybe she'd come over and play in my fort. Maybe her mom would invite me in for baloney sandwiches.

Everything in my little body wanted to be with that girl. But I had competition—another seven-year-old dude named Tom. He lived across the street, and he had all kinds of things that I didn't have. He had a really cute cat, cooler toys, and a mom who made killer little sandwiches, the kind that were too small for a meal, but just the right size for an afternoon snack.

But I loved her. I was sure that she knew it and that she felt the same way. Snack sandwiches and cute cats were no match for our love.

Then one day she broke my heart. We'd all been playing in her front yard—me, Tom, and the girl of my dreams. Both Tom and I did our best to prove ourselves to her. He demonstrated his ability to catch bugs (I've got to admit, he was really good at that). I made whistles, using blades of grass wedged between my thumbs.

Somehow, Tom won out. Whatever it was . . . however he did it,

Tom won her heart. After we'd been playing and showing off for about an hour, she declared that she and Tom would be in love forever . . . and that I needed to go home.

I stayed a failure at dating. The girl always chose the other kid, always ditched me for another guy. Other guys got girls to go out with them—I couldn't. My friends understood things about the opposite sex—I didn't.

It was like that for most of my life. When it came to dating, I always missed the point, was always the last to understand. Along the way, people tried to offer me advice—friends in high school, guys in college, and even in graduate school; I've been helped by the best of the best. It took God's hand—and the right girl—to change my failure at dating into one unbelievable success.

Do you feel like a total failure at dating? Do you need some advice for your dating life? Lots of people have advice about dating. One extreme tells you not to date at all. They give you the "dating is evil" speech and tell you that real Christian students would never date. The other extreme encourages you to date, but gives you no rules or guidelines, leaving that all up to you.

Going Out Without Freaking Out has a different perspective.

I don't think that it's wrong to date. Some people may counsel you to stay away from dating until you're way older and way more mature. But dating isn't unhealthy; it's natural. How do you get to know people of the opposite sex? How do you know how the other sex thinks? How do you get to know people you don't usually hang out with? Through dating. As long as your parents agree that you're ready, dating is totally cool.

If you're not dating already, you soon will be. Maybe not today, and maybe not tomorrow—but you *will* date. From that starting point, you could go in many directions—you can make huge mistakes . . . or you can have some great successes. My hope is that this book will help you be more successful.

Going Out Without Freaking Out deals with the basics. It assumes that you're getting ready to date or are early in your dating experience. Even if you're older, you might be "young" as far as dating is concerned. You won't find advanced advice on marriage, or details about how to say "no" to sex in this book. But you'll get some good advice about navigating your early dating experiences. You'll also be given good date ideas to try out with someone you know, or like, or are interested in. These date ideas give you opportunities to try out the advice in this book.

Oh, and remember, *Going Out Without Freaking Out* is written by a *complete failure at dating*. I've made loads of dating mistakes. I date like I dance—and I'm a very bad dancer. This book lets you learn from my mistakes, and have a good laugh at them. Above all, this book will help you not to be afraid of the opposite sex and not to be afraid of dating.

Dating isn't super easy—but it can be super fun. This book encourages you to understand what your dating life can be, and how you can keep God at the center of every dating encounter.

God bless you as you journey through this book.

One

The Truth About Your Dating Foundation:
God and Your Parents

No one should eat rattlesnake. Cow tongue? Out of the question.

I was once eating lunch with a room full of people from church. We were all having a great time, eating and hanging out. Near the end of the meal, one of the men offered to share some exotic meats that he'd brought.

I don't like to try new meats, and things like "exotic meats" freak me out. So when this guy brought out a few plastic containers, I got nervous. When he opened a container and passed around pieces of cooked rattlesnake, I started to sweat. When the rattlesnake container came to me and people started to *eat* it, my body convulsed in one of those pre-vomit, uncontrollable, puke-like muscle spasms. Just as I passed the rattlesnake (and the laughter over my convulsing grew), the guy said, "Hey, Tim. I've got cow tongue casserole in this other one. Check this out." It was nasty. It was nastier when I noticed that the tongue still had the taste buds on it.

If you like rattlesnake or cow tongue, don't be offended. It's just that those foods seem a bit extreme and kind of weird. Why do people chase after strange food? In a world with hamburgers, pizza, french fries, and steak, why do people choose to eat rattlesnake and cow tongue?

Eating strange foods is something like dating the wrong way. We have access to the best foundation and the best advice for dating we could dream of: the God who created us and who knows us best. He ought to be the source, the fuel, and the foundation for our dating.

But even though we have this awesome foundation, we often rely on other things. If you're completely consumed with having sex, for instance, that becomes your foundation and fuels every dating decision you make. If you want to date only popular people, that foundation filters into every dating decision.

If pleasing God is your only foundation, if that's your fuel, then every dating decision you make will be healthy.

You know what's really strange? We'll pick *anything* other than God, and rely on that thing as our foundation. When we do, we make huge mistakes, the relationship explodes, and we get hurt. But we have something much better to rely upon. We don't have to settle.

If pleasing God is your only foundation, if that's your fuel, then every dating decision you make will be healthy. You'll not only make better decisions, you'll have better dating experiences. Those experiences will be different for each of us, but the most important aspect of dating ought to be the same for all of us—and that's our relationship with God.

We have a second important foundation, as well. Your dating life actually begins long before you begin dating. Before you go out on your first date—possibly before you begin even to notice the opposite sex—you're gaining valuable insight into relationships from your parents.

So you have two important foundations for dating—God and your parents.

The God Foundation

If you don't know God—or if your relationship with him is weak—then your dating life won't be as smooth as it could be. God wants to be the foundation for everything you do, including dating. He wants you to rely upon him, in fact, for every dating decision. But how do you make God the foundation of your dating? Here are a few ideas.

You and God

First, you've got to have a good relationship with God. Without that relationship, not only will your dating life be a wreck, your whole life will be a wreck. Yeah, you could get a lot of dates, you might meet a great person, you might get married and have a good life. But your life won't be everything it could be without a solid relationship with God.

The God Invasion

Having a strong relationship with God, though, isn't enough. Your relationship with God should invade every aspect of every relationship. But God is polite when it comes to invading our lives. We have to seek him out and ask him to guide and direct every step we take in every aspect of our lives. That includes our dating lives and our relationships with the opposite sex.

Listen to God

Just knowing God and inviting him into your every decision still isn't enough. You've also got to listen to him. Not listening to God is like calling someone your best friend, but never talking to them, and never listening to them. God doesn't just want to know you, and he doesn't want you just to keep him in the loop when it comes to your life. He wants to interact with you. He wants to talk with you about everything, including your dating life. How does God speak to us? Primarily through his Word. Want to know what God thinks about your dating life? Read his words to you. Are you spending time listening to God? You'll never know what he wants for you if you're not listening.

The Parent Foundation

Your parents aren't so much the other foundation as they are the foundation upon the foundation. Your parents are the people God often uses to help you know his rules and to plan your life.

Your parents might sometimes do some weird things, but they love you. And your parents are really God's hands in your life. The rules they make and the way they guide you are the ways that they act for God for your benefit. Your parents are God's caretakers of your life. Here are some of the reasons your parents are important for your dating life.

The Gatekeepers

You have to obey your parents and the rules they've set for your dating life and for the relationships you have with the opposite sex. That means if your parents say that you can't date until you're sixteen, that's the rule. If they say you can't stay out later than 9:00 p.m. with someone of the opposite sex, that's the rule. You can look at these rules in a negative way, get depressed, and feel like you can't live your life. Or you could look at your parents as what they are—God's hands in your life, directing and guiding you.

Your parents are God's caretakers of your life.

They Have a History

Whether they fell in love at twelve or met each other later in life, your parents have a dating history. And their dating experiences can help you. Ask them how they've failed at dating. Listen to their successes. Learn everything you can from their experiences. Their history can really help you.

They Love You

Your parents love you. They don't want to do or say anything that would hurt you. They'd never give you advice that would cause you harm. You can rely on their advice, not just because they're probably right, but because they wouldn't steer you wrong. Even if you're away at college or you don't live with your parents, their advice can help you. They can still serve as guides for your dating life.

The Combination of God and Your Parents

Your strong walk with God and your healthy relationship with your parents combine to create a solid foundation for your dating life. God uses your parents to guide you a lot more than you might think. Without these two working together you don't have a reliable foundation. This combined foundation of God and your parents infiltrates every area of your dating life.

There's no other foundation you can build upon for successful dating. Yet we try to build our relationships with the opposite sex on other foundations. We think that just being in a relationship completes our lives, or that having sex with someone is the right way to date. In the end, those foundations are useless and they don't work, and we usually discover that they're useless only after we've experienced a lot of pain.

God's design for dating is so simple. If you rely upon the foundation of God and your parents, you'll be successful.

If Your Foundation Is Broken

You live in the real world, though. Maybe your life doesn't rest securely upon the "God and Your Parents" foundation. You may, in fact, not fit the mold—a fantastic relationship with God, living in a stable home with your biological mom and dad.

No. Very likely your foundation has been broken. Maybe your relationship with God isn't strong. If that's true, I'd suggest talking with your youth pastor about how you can strengthen your walk with God. Until you've got a solid walk with God your dating relationships won't be as great as they could be.

Your life may be affected by divorce, or you see that your parents don't have a healthy relationship, that they're not ideal models to ask for dating advice or for healthy rules for dating. If that's so, I suggest a couple of things.

First, even though your parents are divorced, they still love you and want the best for you. They're still your best place for support, advice, rules, and guidelines for dating. Your parents are still a great foundation for you to rely upon. If they're divorced they probably have some excellent advice about the problems to avoid in relationships. You still need to listen to them, and you still need to obey their rules for dating and relationships.

Second, you might find a couple whose relationship is still intact, and who you can ask for advice about dating. It's not that your parents aren't worth observing, it's just that it helps to have a healthy, connected family as an example for what a relationship could be. Seek out your youth pastor, senior pastor, or another person in your church and observe that person's relationship with his or her spouse. Observing a healthy relationship helps us in our dating relationships.

Building on the Foundation

With God and your parents as your foundation for dating, you won't mess up your life. Yeah, you'll make mistakes. Yeah, your heart will be broken. You'll fall in love with someone who doesn't love you back. But you'll be experiencing all that while relying upon the most solid foundation you could ever have.

What freaks you out about dating the opposite sex?

The foundation of God and your parents is only the start of a good dating life. There are loads of things that are important to understand and learn more about. These include things such as knowing more about yourself, understanding the opposite sex, knowing more about what respect is, not freaking out about the first date. The chapters that follow discuss eleven dating topics that you'll use to build upon your God foundation. The topics are presented in the order that's best for tackling them. First, knowing and understanding yourself helps you relate better to the opposite sex. Then, knowing more about and understanding the opposite sex helps when you date them.

So let's keep moving. What freaks you out about dating the opposite sex? What are you apprehensive about? No doubt you've got some big questions and some things that scare you. The next chapter starts with some of the basics.

→ Connecting with Yourself

- Evaluate how strong your relationship with God is. Do you feel it's strong enough? How could your relationship with God be stronger?

→ Connecting with Your Friends

- Ask your friends to pray with you as you all begin your dating adventure.

→ Connecting with Your Parents

- Ask your parents what they learned about dating from *their* parents. What did they learn from observing their parents? How did their relationship with God affect their dating life?

→ Connecting with God

- Ask God to help you rely upon him for your dating life. As you journey through this book, make it a point to pray through the topics of each chapter, asking God to help you rely upon him more as you date.

Two

The Truth About Dating Basics

It's crunch time. Lindsay has been waiting for Ben to ask her out. Finally, he's got the guts. Here's how it goes.

Ben: "Um . . . hey. I, uhh . . . well . . . I'm going to the movies this weekend."

Lindsay: "Wow, what are you gonna see?"

Ben: "I'm not sure. But, I'd uh . . . I'd hate to go alone. You know."

Lindsay: "Yeah. You shouldn't go alone. Can't you find someone to go with you?"

Ben: "Yeah."

Lindsay: "Well . . . great. I hope you enjoy the movie."

Ben: "Yeah."

Ben looks like he has more to say. He doesn't. Lindsay thought he had the guts. He doesn't. She hoped he'd ask *her* to go to the movie with him. He didn't. Ben walks away . . . still looking like he's got unfinished business racing through his skull. Lindsay walks away . . . so close to a date . . . so close.

What makes dating so difficult?

Why is it so hard to ask someone out?

Why does it seem like torture to go on a date?

Does it have to feel like you're constantly on the sale rack, waiting for someone to take you off your hanger?

Does it have to feel like you're shopping for the best deal?

No! Dating can be great. Going on dates doesn't have to feel like you're at war with the opposite sex. But you've got to know some important stuff before you set out to date someone. How does the other person think? How do you treat your date? What do you do if you have a big, nasty glob of food stuck in your teeth? What if you trip and fall in the mud, and it splashes all over your date? What if your date stands up in the middle of McDonald's, points at you, and screams, "This person is a nerd and *everyone* needs to know that," and then walks out.

Dating doesn't have to freak you out. Dating can be a great thing that leads to experiences and relationships you'll always remember. By dating, you learn a lot about yourself. You learn about the opposite sex. You even learn about God. But so many things about dating are freaky, you can feel overwhelmed.

The Short History of Dating

Dating as we know it today is not as old as you think. I'm not talking about arranged marriages and stuff like that. I mean having the freedom to take an interest in whomever we choose and follow up on it. In our part of the world, dating became popular in the early 1900s. Back then, parents were very involved in whom their teenager could "court" or be "courted" by, where they could meet (mostly in the girl's home), and what they would do. So dating was more of an "arrangement," with the parents putting restrictions on their kids.

In the higher classes, a girl's parents took more interest in the financial level of the guy's parents, and the guy's parents were concerned about the social level of the girl's parents. They weren't especially concerned about whether or not the two young people actually liked each other. Parents just wanted their kids to make a "respectable" match.

The "lower classes," though, didn't take the same things into consideration as the higher classes (or have the socially acceptable "parlor" room to visit in). So their kids "went out" with their courters or court-ees. Hence, the idea of a "date."

Dating Advice from Your Parents

Here's a test.

Nate just asked Kelsie to go out with him this weekend. He's excited. One problem—Nate didn't ask his parents if he could go *anywhere* this weekend.

He's stuck.

You might feel like you could write this section. You may have already talked with your folks about dating. Or you may be avoiding it because you think you know what they'll say, and you really don't want to hear it again. Your parents may be the last people you want to hear from about dating. But be assured—they know a whole lot about it because they've been there (and lived to tell about it). That's worth something, right?

Imagine for a moment that you are the parent, and that your parents are your kids.

Your parents love you, and while their way of showing it may seem overprotective and strange, they *do* love you. They don't want you to be hurt, in danger, or even mildly troubled in any way. They know that you're bound to experience some hurt, and that dating is one thing that can bring pain into your life. But to help you avoid at least some of the pain, they'll do whatever they can.

That's love. And while their need to protect may not always seem like a direct expression of love, it's them telling you they would tread water for days in the Bering Sea (it's cold there, trust me) if it would keep you safe and happy.

Honestly.

Let's play a little role reversal. Imagine for a moment that you are the parent, and that your parents are your kids. They've just approached you and asked if it's okay to go on a date. This being their first date, you want to give them some advice. Knowing what you know about being a young person, and thinking about some of the things they need to watch out for, what advice might you give them? Take a minute right now and think about that. What advice would you give to yourself? Go ahead, take your time . . . I'll wait.

See? You've got advice. And you wouldn't offer your advice unless you cared about the person you're giving it to. Well your parents care about you, and they've got advice, too.

Your parents have probably experienced (in some form) all the stuff you're going through—including dating. Yeah, your parents have had dating experiences. They've been there, done that. They've cried. Their hearts have been broken. They've felt massively in love. They've panicked over what to wear (and argued with *their* parents over what they *weren't* allowed to wear). Dating is new to you, but not to them. It's cool, then, that you have someone who's already gone through it and is there to help you.

You have only one heart—don't give it away easily.

What advice might your parents give you about dating? Every parental unit is different, but here are a few things they'd probably want to say.

Ain't no do-overs. Your parents would probably want to tell you that they regret rushing through their teen years, because they didn't take time to enjoy them and learn more from them. This piece of advice usually begins with, "When I was your age . . ." and probably includes advice like "take it easy"; "remember to have fun"; and best of all, "you've got your whole life ahead of you." What your parents want you to know is: resist the urge to grow up quickly. You'll only be sixteen for a year. Enjoy yourself. Don't rush. There's no reason to rush into dating, and there's no reason to be in a hurry to go out with anyone. Go slowly. Be patient.

Stand guard over your heart. You have only one heart—don't give it away easily. This sounds like another cliché, but think about it. You have the opportunity to give your heart to anyone. Make sure the person you give it to respects you and treats you well. You may always try to see the best in people, and you might think your date has some great qualities, but people aren't always what they seem. Be selective about who you choose to trust.

Friendships can turn into amazing relationships. I know it doesn't sound thrilling, but developing a friendship with someone before you start dating that person builds a terrific foundation. You become comfortable with that person and can rest assured that he or she is interested in *you* and not your looks or your stuff. And you might have more fun with that person and feel less self-conscious—you're with someone that you already have this great friendship with.

You're not an adult...not yet! No doubt your parents are probably thrilled to see how you've grown into a teenager. But dating can put you in situations where you're pressured to rebel against what you know is right. You'll face situations where you'll be tempted to go against what your parents have taught you. You'll feel pressured to go against what you know the Bible says you should do, or how you should act. Guess what. Your parents lay down rules for you, not to torture you, but to help you learn how to make good decisions. Those rules aren't there to make you feel less adult; they're there to help you become a happy adult!

Let's talk. Your parents *need* to know you're okay. And if you're not, they want to help you. Your parents want to answer your questions, and they want to know all of your fears about dating. They *want* to talk to you. Talking, though, takes two people. Don't expect your parents to climb inside your head and find out your questions for themselves. *Talk* to your parents. Let them know everything you're feeling and experiencing in your dating life.

Dating Advice from the Bible

One day you decide to get some facts about dating from the Bible. You go to your handy-dandy concordance and open it to the "D" section. Nothing.

No problem. You head to your handy Bible dictionary, go to the "D" section.

Nothing.

This is ridiculous. As a last-ditch effort, you go to the Internet, type in your favorite search engine, and enter "Dating in the Bible."

What do you get? A bunch of weird Bible study sites, and a few wacko websites devoted to Bible prophecy.

Stumped? Fact is, God's Word doesn't specifically mention dating. God didn't give Moses the Ten Commandments of Dating. And the apostle Paul didn't write a letter to any church about their dating practices. So you're left with looking at the lives of Bible characters. There are loads of pretty cool people in the Bible who went on dates. And through their dating habits, we get a good picture of God's initial advice for how to date.

Here are a few real-life examples of dating from the Bible.

Isaac and Rebekah. In Genesis 24, Isaac's dad decides that Isaac needs a wife. He sends one of his servants to his old stomping ground in Nahor to find the right woman for Isaac.

This sounds like a typical arranged-marriage story, but keep reading.

The servant goes, and in his concern for finding the right woman, he prays to God: "Lead me to the right woman for Isaac." The servant is resting by a spring in the evening when the women of the village come to draw their water. He notices one—a beautiful young girl named Rebekah. He prays, "God let me know who the right girl is in this way: When I ask one of them for a drink, she'll offer water to me and also offer to give water to my camels." When the servant approaches Rebekah, she does exactly that!

Above everything else in all of your relationships and friendships, God wants you to love others as he loves you.

Rebekah invites the servant to meet her family and have dinner. But before they eat, he explains the whole amazing story to them.

They're happy to give their daughter in marriage, and she's happy to go.

When Isaac sees her arriving with the servant, he immediately falls for her. Verse 67 says, "Isaac brought her into the tent of his mother Sarah, and he married Rebekah. So she became his wife, and he loved her."

Arranged marriages aren't the same as just dating, but the story tells us an important characteristic about God: He can intervene by sending certain people into your life. And if you pray about it, God will hear your prayer. You can pray that God will lead you to people—the right people—to have friendships and dating relationships with. And as this story shows, he'll do it if that's his will.

Jacob and Rachel. In Genesis 29:9–20, Jacob falls madly in love with Rachel. Her family requires him to work for them seven years before he can marry her. But check this out. Verse 20 says the seven years "seemed like only a few days to him because of his love for her." This short story demonstrates the devotion that we often feel toward someone we've fallen for.

These days, guys don't have to work as a slave in the home of their date's parents, but the lesson of this story still applies. Jacob shows Rachel and her family devotion and respect.

Above everything else in all of your relationships and friendships, God wants you to love others as he loves you.

What does that mean? How does God let you know that he loves you?

It can be summed up in one word: Jesus. God sent his Son, Jesus, to earth to die for our sins. And he did that because God loves us endlessly, immeasurably, incredibly. We are all born sinners, and without God's forgiveness we're dead. But Jesus' sacrificial death on the cross changed that. All those who believe in Jesus as Savior and believe in God's saving grace through Jesus' death and resurrection have eternal life.

Now that's the definition of love! And that life-giving love should be the reason we love other people. And love should be the reason we live by God's commands and guidelines in our relationships. (Chapter 9,

"Affection," details info about the Bible's advice on how to conduct yourself with the opposite sex.)

The Burning Questions

You've probably got *huge* questions about dating. You're not alone. No one has the dating thing figured out. For most of us, dating is an unending learning experience. If you have questions about any aspect of dating, ask your parents or your pastor. While this book helps you navigate many of the rough spots in your dating life, it won't help you with all of them. And nothing substitutes for the advice of your parents and your pastor. As you read through this book, take your questions to an adult who will give you complete answers, and will guide you through your dating life.

It's totally cool to ask your friends for their dating ideas and suggestions. Just remember—most of your friends are as clueless as you are. And their parents' rules about dating might not be the same as your family's. Yeah, your friends act like they know everything about dating. Yeah, they'll give you answers that sound great. But lots of times they don't really know what's going on. Fire your questions at them, but be sure to ask your parents or your pastor the same questions, just to get other opinions.

"Is dating okay for me at this point in my life?"

Asking your parents, or pastor, or friends might be a huge help. No doubt you've got a lot of questions you might want to ask. Here are a few questions (and answers) to get you started.

Is dating okay? The majority of teens today would probably laugh at that question, thinking, "This isn't the Stone Age—of course dating is okay!" But the answer to that question isn't the same for everyone. The question should be, "Is dating okay for me at this point in my life?" How do you answer that? The truth is, no one but you, your parents, and God can give you the answer.

Think, though, about what your answer to that question would be. Other concerns in your life right now—scholastic goals, other activities you're involved in, maybe even family anxieties—may make dating seem too overwhelming. Ask yourself, "Is now a good time for me to be dating?" Don't base the answer just on what you want or what you feel, but on what you think is the right decision.

What age is the right age to date? This is one that you need to discuss with your parents. Some teens are allowed to date at twelve years old, some not until sixteen years old, and different dating guidelines apply for every age in between. Some parents might feel that group dates are okay but not alone dates, or escorted dates but not car dates. Each type of dating is different, and that's why you should talk this over with your folks.

What kinds of things are okay to do on a date? Your parents probably have limits for the kinds of places you're allowed to go and the kind of people you're allowed to hang with. Ask them what boundaries they have for you and your dating life. If your parents don't have specific rules to guide you, it's okay to rely on your own internal sense of right and wrong. Some things you do or places you go on a date won't feel right—listen to yourself. Remember, group dates are okay. Saying "no" to where your date wants to take you is okay. Talk to your parents, pastor, and friends about the places you ought to go on a date.

Dating a non-Christian can seriously hinder your walk with God.

Is it okay to date non-Christians? No. Don't try it. You and a nonbeliever don't share some of the basic views of life. You don't have the same values. And, most importantly, your destiny isn't anything alike. Dating a non-Christian can seriously hinder your walk with God. Don't do it.

Is falling in love okay at my age? You know the problem with a dating book, dating philosophies, and a lot of the dating advice you probably get? They never tell you how important it is to fall in love. Is it possible to fall in love as a teenager? Yes. With God and your parents guiding you, falling in love is totally okay. Remember, above all the dating philosophy and advice you'll get, falling in love is part of the purpose of dating.

As you read this book you'll find more complete answers to these questions. As you encounter questions about your dating life, remember—there's more than one answer to each question. Different people will give you different answers. Choose carefully the people you ask for help and ideas. Who should you talk to? Always talk to your parents first—they love you, and they will probably give you the best advice (remember . . . they're part of your essential foundation!). Your pastor or youth pastor can give you excellent advice about dating too. If you've got good, close friends who have already dated, consider asking them for dating advice. Sometimes, a good friend can give you great advice.

And, remember—everyone dates differently. No two people look at dating in the same way. Some of us know exactly what to do on dates. Others of us need a little help. Do you wish that each time you went on a date you knew exactly what to do? Knew all the right things to say or all the right ways to act? It's impossible to get *everything* right, and it's impossible to know *everything* about dating. But getting the basics down is essential. The first part of this book lays the groundwork, and so far we've covered just a few of the basics. So what's next?

You—you're next. You've got to work on yourself. Before you can go out with the opposite sex, you've got to know more about yourself. You need to feel comfortable about who you are before you go on a date. So the next chapter asks you to look honestly at who you are.

→ Connecting with Yourself

- Make a list of the things about dating that scare you. Evaluate your readiness. Ask yourself, "Am I really ready to go on a date?"

→ **Connecting with Your Friends**

- Ask your friends if they're afraid to date. If they say they are, ask them what scares them about dating.

→ **Connecting with Your Parents**

- Ask your parents if they had any fears about dating when they were your age. Ask your parents what advice they might have for you about overcoming your dating fears.

→ **Connecting with God**

- Ask God to help you feel secure and ready to date. Ask God to prepare the people you will be dating. Ask him to join you with the right person.

Three

The Truth About You

Mrs. Jordan needs some egg rolls and rice for the international dinner at church. She takes her son, David, and his friend Adam with her to the store. As soon as they enter, Dave and Adam break away from Mrs. J, promising to meet her at the checkout. Dave and Adam make their way to the huge magazine rack and look through the computer magazines. After a while, Adam notices one magazine with an extremely good looking young woman on the cover. "D-u-ude!" says Adam. "She is hot!"

Dave and Adam gawk at the cover. After a few seconds of lust-filled silence, they comment on the cover, the woman on the cover, and the things they were feeling. Let's just say that their comments probably weren't the nicest.

As Adam drools on himself and Dave burns holes in the magazine with his eyes, they feel a presence behind them. Standing there, looking at Dave and Adam going crazy over the magazine in their hands, is Mrs. J. She's wearing one of those parental embarrassed looks.

And Dave and Adam feel really weird.

It doesn't take much searching today to get a picture of what pop culture calls beautiful. Television, the Net, and magazines all paint the picture of "the perfect person." Want to be attractive? Modern culture says you have to be thin, tan, blue eyed, and athletic. Want to be popular? You've got to be "good looking" *and* outgoing, play sports, wear designer clothes.

So where does that leave you? If you don't fit pop culture's mold, you probably feel ugly. If you're not outgoing, you might not feel popular. If your clothes come from K-Mart, you probably feel like a geek.

The average American is not the image portrayed on the cover of a magazine or in a music video.

Not feeling attractive, not being popular, and not wearing designer labels can work out to a pretty awful equation. It goes like this:

Feeling ugly + feeling unpopular + feeling geeky = feeling like a useless outcast

When you don't fit the mold, you question your own value. You doubt your own worth. You think that you'll never be accepted anywhere, that you'll never be loved by anyone other than your parents and God. You believe that you'll never accomplish anything in this world.

The average American is not the image portrayed on the cover of a magazine or in a music video. A silent war is being waged today. On one side are the normal looking, normal acting people—people who'd feel okay about themselves if it weren't for the people on the other side. On the other side are people who want to tell you what beautiful is. They print magazines, they make television shows, they preach to you in all kinds of media. The message? You have to look a certain way. You have to act a certain way. And if you don't look or act in "the right way," then you have no value.

Truth is, you're being lied to. You don't need me to tell you that; you already know it. So let's just come right out and say it:

Magazines Are Big Fat Liars

Girls, magazines want you to believe that to be beautiful your body has to be trim. Guys, magazines want you to believe that unless you've got six-pack-abs, you'll never go out with any girl.

But even as you read this, there's a voice in your head probably saying, "But I *would* be popular if I were thinner, or taller, or had a different nose, or were more muscular. And I'd have more friends if I dressed like a rock star."

Look, all those lies are just that—lies. Magazines want you to believe that they are *the* word on what you must strive for, and that they hold the key to achieving it. They claim that they're only representing what the rest of society says is desirable. Not true. They're liars. They are lying to you.

Television and Movies Want to Deceive You

Equally as guilty as magazines are the TV shows, movies, video games, music videos, and other media that present body forms and face arrangements that are "perfect." Such media represent the owners of these perfect forms as people to be admired. And then these media report the questionable morals and behavior of these same people. It's like they're saying, "If you're this pretty or handsome (and you should be), you can act this way."

Oh, I know. Media doesn't explicitly *say* that some people aren't good looking or popular. But it implies it by not showing you a representation of what real people with real bodies look like. Do you ever see less-than-thin people dancing on music videos? Nope. Do you ever see not-so-thin people modeling bathing suits? No. That omission adds up to a lie. If media doesn't show you what real people look like—showing you a select group of people instead—that's a lie.

Your Friends Don't Get It

And what's the most difficult part of this? Your friends. Yeah, you love them. Yeah, they love you. But what's worse? A magazine that lies, or a friend who believes the lie? It's tough when a friend we love believes this stuff, spends their time trying to look "perfect," and tells us that we need to look perfect too.

It's worse when our friend says that, along with looking perfect, our behavior must copy that of popular people. We have to go out, drink, party because that's what we're *supposed* to do. We have to wear certain clothes, have a certain attitude, do the right things in order to be beautiful, popular, and successful.

Your friends who believe this don't get it. They don't get that they're being deceived. Don't listen to them.

A few pages ago, I gave you this equation:

Feeling ugly + feeling unpopular + feeling geeky = feeling like a useless outcast

When you look at the previous three statements about the media and your friends, the math gets even more damaging. Why? Because along with these lies, the world offers ways you can fix the "problems" you supposedly have. Is your chest too small? Get implants. Is your belly too big? Get liposuction. Are you introverted? See a shrink or take a pill.

Those lies distract you from becoming who God made you to be.

See? You're not only whacked around by a false set of standards, you're also offered false solutions that could possibly hurt you. I'm *not* saying that you shouldn't read magazines. I'm *not* saying that you should never watch television, movies, or music videos. And you *should* hang out with your friends. But you need to know that the media aren't giving you a picture of what real people look like. And if you don't fit the mold marketed by the media, you can feel really, really bad about yourself.

But you are *wonderful.* Do you realize why those lies are so bad? Not just because they're lies, but because those lies distract you from becoming who God made you to be. Every time you believe the lie, it's like saying, "Because I don't look a certain way, God made me less than perfect, so God didn't do a good job making me." He did do a good job. He did a perfect job. God is not lying to you when He says you're great just the way you are. God doesn't want you to fit into any mold; he wants you to be the person he created you to be.

What God Says

So, ask yourself, "What *is* normal?" If the people you see in magazines and movies don't represent the normal person, what does? How do you know if you're normal?

If you're you, you're normal. The way you look, the way your face is arranged, your body shape—all of that is good and normal, and you're extremely good looking. "But," you say, "you don't know me. How can you say that *I'm* normal and that my face arrangement and body shape are good?"

Simple. God says it. Go with me through some Scripture.

Read Genesis chapters 1 and 2. You'll see that God created everything. After God molded man and woman with his hands, he said, "This is very good." Not just good—*very good.* Don't miss the significance of two things. First, God did the work. The creator of everything worked his hardest and created humans. He made them. He formed them. Second, God was pleased with his work on the first humans. He loved what he did.

In Psalm 139, David writes his inner thoughts about his life and his understanding of who God is. He writes, "You formed me." David acknowledges what Adam and Eve already knew. God continues to make humans, and as his creation, we watch it happen. We watch a pregnant mother's stomach enlarge, and we can see the growth of a baby through sonogram machines. And it's God who is doing the work.

God decides what real, ultimate, true beauty is.

You were once that baby being formed by God's hands. And you aren't just God's work, you are God's *very good* work. God looks at you and is pleased with the work he's done, making you who you are.

Why do we let other people tell us what beauty is? Why do we listen to media or our friends who tell us what the perfect face is or the right body shape looks like? Let me ask you a few questions.

- Ultimately, is anyone's opinion about you more important than God's?
- Could anyone care more about you than God?
- Could anyone know more about beauty than God?

God decides what real, ultimate, true beauty is. He *loves* the way you look, because, according to Scripture, you bear a striking resemblance to him. And God likes not just the way you look, he likes the way you are. He loves your personality, he loves your laugh, he loves the way you look in the morning.

I never fully understood the extent of God's love until I had children. When Jacqui and I found out we were going to have our first child, I was a bit nervous. I wasn't ready to spend a lot of nights getting very little sleep, and I didn't look forward to changing diapers. All my nervousness went away when I saw the birth of our first child. The moment I saw her I totally understood what God's parental, unconditional love is like. As they've grown, my kids are always beautiful, and fun, and interesting. I think that's how God views us. Because we are his creation, God loves us . . . he always loves us.

God loves you. Always. No matter if you're wearing the latest styles, no matter if you're popular, if you're the star of the soccer team, if you have one good friend or a thousand. But let's be honest. Sometimes it doesn't matter how much you know about God's love. If you feel rotten about yourself, God's love can feel a million miles away. Before you'll be a success at dating, you've got to grasp how wonderfully created you are, and you've got to understand how much God loves you. Until you understand how perfect your face, body, and personality are you'll always search for a fix for your body or you'll want to change something about yourself. Until you understand how much God loves you the way you are, you'll search for forever until someone loves you. And you'll probably find someone who'll love you for who you could be—but not for who you are.

Until you grasp how much God loves you and how wonderfully created you are, you'll never be a success at dating. You'll have relationships, but they won't be fulfilling. You'll find clothes that fit, but you'll never be happy in them. You're great just the way you are. God loves you. Understand that—before you seriously consider dating.

You

Think about who you are. You're a combination of your parent's looks, your family's temperament, the way you were raised, and lots of other things. You're a product of body chemistry, how much sleep you got last night, how you feel about yourself, and how you think others feel about you.

Let's have a one-person pep rally. Take a few moments and get it all out. How do you feel about yourself? What are your strengths? Read these questions and answer them in your mind.

• What is my best physical feature?
• What do I like the best about my face?
• What do I like the best about my body?
• What do I like best about my personality?
• What's the best thing about being me?
• What am I good at?
• What do others compliment me about?
• If God were complimenting me, what might he say?

Begin believing that you are an awesome creation of God.

How did you do? I hope those questions helped you discover a few positive things about yourself that you've never thought of. After you reject the lies that the world crams down your throat and better understand how wonderful you are, what's your next step? Begin trusting in who you are. Begin believing that you are an awesome creation of God—and live like you believe it. You're great looking. You're great to be around. People like you. Believe it!

Right now you may be saying, "I feel great about myself. I look okay, and I'm not insecure about my personality or abilities." Great! But many of us too easily believe the lies about looks and personality. When you're tempted to believe them, remember—what God says about you is the truth.

Finding Another Awesome Person Like You

So God loves you, and you're great. That'd be wonderful if dating was a one-person thing, but it isn't. It takes two people to form a great dating relationship. So although we're talking about you right now, let's think beyond you for a bit. Not only were you created to love and worship God; you were created to be in a relationship with someone. What kind of person would you fit best with? What should that other person be like? Knowing what you're like, what should the *other* person be like?

First, you need a standard. A standard is a rule or guideline that tells you what kind of person you ought to consider dating. Why is a standard such a big deal? Because now you understand that you're not junk, and that who you are is really, really great. It's important to think about what kind of person would complement you. Use the questions below to think about your standards for the person that you want to date.

- What kind of person would best fit me?
- What kind of person would I be most comfortable dating?
- What values does the person I date need to have?
- What kind of personality do I want the person whom I date to have?

After you assemble the basic standards for the kind of person you'd like to date, form in your head a list of qualities (like physical things or personality traits) you'd like your potential date to have. List some things that your potential date might do, say, or think. If you're not sure about the above list, ask others about the kind of person they think you ought to date. Remember, your parents probably know you better than anyone else on earth does. They know your strengths and weaknesses. They know the kind of person you might fit with. Also, your friends are great people to ask about the kind of people you might best fit with. Your friends know a side of you that most other people don't. They know what makes you laugh, and they know the people who go to your school. They might be able to help you choose someone who would be a good fit for you.

All right. We've got a handle on *you*. You've thought about your value to God, how much you honor yourself, what you consider beautiful in looks and character. You've established some standards for the kind of person you'd date. But before you'll be completely comfortable with dating you've got to understand some things about the opposite sex. What makes them tick? Read the next chapter to find out more.

➔ Connecting with Yourself

- Make a list of things about yourself that you feel insecure about. Make another list of your positive qualities. Read through both lists several times. Pray through these lists, asking God to help you feel secure about yourself.

➔ Connecting with Your Friends

- Talk with your friends about how they feel about themselves. Ask them to share one area in which they feel insecure about themselves.

➔ Connecting with Your Parents

- Ask your parents to share their insecurities with you. You might begin by saying, "When you were my age, what were you insecure about?" Then ask your parents to tell you the things they like about you.

→ Connecting with God

- Ask God to help you ignore the media lies about what is beautiful. Ask God to help you feel secure with how he has created and formed you, and about who he has made you to be.

Four

The Truth About the Opposite Sex

Do aliens exist?

I bet you've thought about it. Everyone has. Are all the other planets in all the other galaxies empty? Do aliens explore the universe in silver spaceships? Do they buzz the Earth, studying our life-forms and reading our minds?

When I was younger I was sure alien life-forms existed. But these "aliens" didn't ride around in spaceships and they weren't mind readers. They had long hair and higher voices. They had cooties. They were weird. They were girls. Later in my life, girls were even weirder. The older I got, the stranger they got. I'm not unusual, either. I've talked to loads of girls who thought the same way about guys.

When we understand how different we are, we can better glorify him in our dating relationships.

Guys and girls are different, and they're different for a reason. God has designed us to be different, and when we understand how different we are, we can better glorify him in our dating relationships.

Stuff You Already Know—God's Chemical Bath

Guys and girls aren't just biologically different, they're emotionally and mentally different, too. But none of these differences are important to us until our bodies and brains are washed with chemicals called hormones. Until then, the only difference we notice about each other is the way we dress, our haircuts, and the obvious physical differences.

When we're little kids, those biological differences aren't important to us. But when those hormones are released we undergo some changes, and the sexes become very different. We even begin thinking and feeling differently. This chemical change (called puberty) begins at different ages and in different ways for each person. It affects each of us differently, and each of us responds differently to the changes.

Puberty is when we begin to *really* notice the differences in the opposite sex—and we like what we see. That's part of the chemical change inside of you. It's God's way both to change you and to give you the desire for the opposite sex. All of the sudden the boys who were stinky don't look so nasty, and the girls who played with dolls aren't so weird. Now, after several years of ignoring the opposite sex, you want to hang out with them.

Basic Differences

The changes that God's chemicals bring to our bodies seem a lot like a non-stop series of nuclear explosions. The changes are huge. They make your body hurt, and they make you constantly feel weird and unsure of what's going on. Some of the results of these changes are easy to notice. Here's a list of the major differences between guys and girls. These categories are only generalizations. You might not fit these descriptions, but that doesn't make you weird. We're all different, and none of us fits neatly into a mold.

Physical differences: Like you need someone to point that out. If you're past the age of fourteen you no doubt see and feel those differences. Even experts on human development don't have as much information as you do because you're actually living the difference right now.

Emotional differences: Guys tend to be emotionally stoic, and girls emotionally open and honest. In general, girls are more in touch with their emotions. How do you know? Simple. Watch a sad movie about a relationship gone bad, or a romantic movie where the couple lives happily ever after. How do girls respond? They cry. Guys usually respond with, "They could have blown more things up in that movie."

Mental differences: Guys and girls process information differently. Girls process information based on how they feel or how the information makes them feel. Guys are analytical and process information as just facts and figures.

By knowing the physical, emotional, mental, and sexual differences between guys and girls, you realize that the sexes approach relationships differently.

Sexual differences: Sexuality is, in fact, the area in which guys and girls are the most different. Your sexuality isn't just a physical process, and it's not just the explosion of chemicals; it's emotional and mental as well. For both guys and girls, sexuality involves mental thoughts and images, emotional feelings, and physical sensations. Girls and guys process these thoughts, feelings, and sensations differently, however, and respond to them differently. Girls' sexual responses are primarily based upon emotion, and to become aroused girls usually need some kind of emotional security. Guys' responses are primarily physical, and they are aroused mostly by touch and by how someone looks.

How does this information help you? How do you apply all these differences between guys and girls to dating? By knowing the physical, emotional, mental, and sexual differences between guys and girls, you realize that the sexes approach relationships differently. And all of us—because of our emotional and sexual differences—date for different reasons, process a date differently, and respond as individuals to our dates.

The Results of These Differences

How do the differences between males and females work out in a dating situation? Here are a few examples that might help you understand.

Jack and Laney

Jack and Laney are standing at the door of Laney's house. They're facing each other, and Jack is holding each of Laney's hands in his. He's gently rubbing her hands with his fingers.

How might Jack and Laney be reading this situation differently? Leap into their heads for a moment.

Jack: "Oh dude, I'm actually touching her! I can't believe how incredible her hands feel. They're soooo soft. I want to kiss her . . . I'm going to kiss her . . . Kiss her you idiot!"

Laney: "I can't believe how romantic this is. His eyes are soooo expressive. It's so sweet the way he's holding my hands. I hope he asks me out again. Maybe he'll kiss me."

Jack and Laney demonstrate the classic difference between guys and girls, and how they perceive a romantic situation. Guys are physically and visually stimulated—and that usually leads to sexual feelings. Girls respond emotionally, appreciating the effort, the mood, and the romantic element of the moment.

Jessica and Chris

Jessica has been listening to Chris's unending dialogue on the book of Romans. Chris thinks that the more he talks about the Bible, the more spiritual he sounds. Jessica just sits and listens.

What's going on in their minds?

Chris: "Maaaaan, I am *spiritual!* Now she has to like me. She's impressed . . . really, really impressed. This'll definitely score me more kissing time."

Jessica: "He's so spiritual. What a man of God. Wow."

The differences in how Chris and Jessica view this situation might not be related to sexual differences as much as to personality differences. In general, however, guys search the whole world for women they can impress. Christian guys aren't any different, but they often spiritualize this process; that is, they act spiritual or quote lots of Bible verses. Look out girls. Guys will sometimes use a spiritual-looking approach to impress you and get you to lower your guard.

Girls, in general, tend to be better listeners. Jessica sits patiently, not necessarily because she wants to learn more about the book of Romans, but because she's wired to be more patient than Chris is.

Luke and Rebecca

Luke and Rebecca are out for a nice dinner. At least Luke thinks it's a nice dinner. For their two-month anniversary, Luke has taken Rebecca to what he thinks is a great restaurant. The table is greasy, the food is cold, and Rebecca hates hamburgers. Their internal dialogue might go something like this:

Luke: "I am obviously the best guy she's ever dated. I rock. I am so cool. Other boyfriends could learn how to treat women from me."

Rebecca: "What a jerk. This is our last date."

The key to understanding the differences in the opposite sex can be wrapped up in one word. Awareness.

Are guys just slobs and like it that way? Are girls just hard to please? Not exactly. Guys, you might not recognize it, but girls actually appreciate it when guys think about them and the kind of romantic meal they might like. Some girls love hamburgers and fries, and the whole atmosphere that comes with that. Others might appreciate a slightly different atmosphere.

The key to understanding the differences in the opposite sex can be wrapped up in one word.

Awareness.

I'm not asking you to become experts in the subject of the opposite sex. It's not important that you know everything about them. I don't want you to become a teenage psychologist, explaining to everyone how special and unique each person is. I am suggesting, however, that you become aware of the differences between the sexes.

When you understand the differences, you're less likely to offend or become offended. You're less likely to create confusion, thinking that your date feels, thinks, and reacts the same way that you do. You're also *more* likely to be successful with the opposite sex when you know and understand as much as you can about them.

Think of it this way: When you're standing on the porch with your date, and she gets mad that you're not getting the romance of the moment; when your boyfriend doesn't understand why you don't want McDonalds for your two-month anniversary dinner—when these tension-filled moments happen, you'll realize they happen because guys and girls understand things differently. As a result of that realization, you won't make a huge mistake because you don't get your date's reaction.

The Dark Side of Chemicals

The differences between guys and girls aren't all cute. They aren't all neat and tidy and easily solved by just understanding the differences between the sexes. The whole hormone thing can make you think and do some really freaky stuff. The hormones raging through your body can cause you to make some serious mistakes and make you feel almost completely out of control. What should you be watching out for?

Lust. The problem with all the chemicals racing through your body is that you're too young to know how to control what's happening. The chemicals running around inside you make you think sexual thoughts about the opposite sex.

Pornography. This one's especially tough for guys. Chemicals can lead to lust. When lust is allowed to go unchecked it can lead you straight to self-gratification—including pornography.

**Your best line of defense is to daily ask
God to help you control yourself.**

Physically Pushy. What happens when you fill a balloon too full with water? It eventually bursts. The same goes with hormones and your body. When you allow hormones to rule over you, they can take over. And when you give them a chance to take over, they will. They can cause you to touch someone and push yourself onto someone in a sexual way, and cause the other person serious emotional and physical harm.

Unchecked chemicals can rule you and ruin your relationship with your date. How do you keep yourself under control? Your best line of defense is to daily ask God to help you control yourself. Ask him to help you ignore sinful thoughts. Also, consider meeting with a friend or pastor or anyone you feel could help you control the results of your raging hormones.

Now that you understand the opposite sex a little better, you're ready to begin building a friendship that might lead to dating. Keep reading and you'll learn more about how to do that.

→ Connecting with Yourself

- Read through the differences between the sexes that were outlined in this chapter. Commit to watching the opposite sex and understanding as much as you can about the way they think and act.

→ Connecting with Your Friends

- Ask your friends what differences they notice between themselves and the opposite sex. Ask your friends if they've ever been in a weird situation that involved not understanding the opposite sex.

→ Connecting with Your Parents

- Ask your parents what they've learned about the differences between guys and girls.

→ Connecting with God

- Ask God to help you understand the differences between you and the opposite sex.

Five

The Truth About Friendship and Dating

I love house shopping with my wife. When we're bored—or want a cheap date—we'll grab a coke and go for a drive. We love driving in neighborhoods, looking at homes. I love the architecture and the way a house sits on its property.

Before we bought our home, we went house-looking like crazy. We were shopping for a home, but we also just enjoyed looking at the houses in our town. One day, we found an unbelievable deal. This large home had huge rooms, a great landscape job, and an impressive exterior. Jacqui and I didn't have to talk it over much—we both wanted that house.

The question was, could we afford such a nice place? When we got home, I immediately called the real estate agent and told her that we were interested in the house.

"Yeah," said the agent. "I know the house. It looks great, doesn't it? It's a real steal. It's listed for twenty-five thousand."

I'm no expert, but that house could have easily sold for way over $100,000. But before I could say anything, the agent continued.

"They're not showing the house to anyone who isn't extremely motivated. And they'll only sell to people who have the cash in hand. The home has to sell as soon as possible, and the owners want the money immediately."

Finally, the agent took a breath.

"Why is such a nice home going so cheaply?" I asked. "This home could easily sell for four times the asking price. What's the deal?"

The agent was quick to answer. "The home looks really good, but there's a problem with the way the foundation was poured. The cement wasn't properly laid. In the past few years, water has seeped into the foundation, and the previous owners either didn't care or couldn't fix the problem. The result is a useless home. The owners want to unload it to someone who wants to salvage some of the materials, level the home, and rebuild on the lot. The home that's there now is completely useless."

Imagine that. A great looking home that's totally broken and useless. A foundation so badly constructed that the home—although expensive and well built—couldn't survive.

That home is a perfect example of how a good relationship with God supports a dating relationship. You can build a dating relationship on a lot of things. And many Christians who date feel that if they merely believe in God they have instant access to a great relationship with the opposite sex. But to have a great dating life, you need more than merely to *believe* in God. You need to have a great *relationship* with God. Likewise, to build a great dating relationship with a person, you begin with a good, strong friendship with that person.

Let's say you love looking your best, and you want to date a person who always looks his or her best. You don't care about the person's personal beliefs as much as you care about the way that person looks. Sure, you want to like who that person is, but you're really, really interested in someone who looks good—always. The person has got to be fit and has to dress well.

Or what if you choose to date someone who's motivated to make a difference in the world. You want to go out with someone who wants to change the world in some way, and someone who will do whatever he or she can do to make a difference. Yeah, you want to go out with someone you can get along with, but more than anything, you want a motivated person.

Both of those qualities are really good. And you could plug in other qualities in the place of the ones mentioned. You might want to go out with someone who wants to work in the ministry, or someone who's really kind to everyone. But before you can build a great dating relationship with a person, you need to establish a friendship with that person.

Building a dating relationship on expectations or performance or even goals or good intentions is like building a house on a bad foundation.

Why? Because beyond who that person wants to become, and way beyond who you want that person to be, you'll want to like him or her. Consider that you may be spending a lot of time with this person. You'll go to movies and out for snacks. Your parents will meet him or her. You'll get to know the person well—how that person feels about school, and music, and health food.

Building a dating relationship on *expectations* or *performance* or even *goals* or *good intentions* is like building a house on a bad foundation. No matter how good the house is, the bad foundation will wreck the entire structure.

Think about a person who's your good friend. What do you know about that person? Everything? Probably. We all have a good friend that we know everything about. We all have a good friend who knows everything about us. That foundation of friendship has probably carried you through all kinds of situations. You've probably had a fight or two, but you've likely come back together. Why? Because you're friends. Your friendship is the glue that keeps you together through some tough moments. If you're going to have a successful dating relationship, you need that same glue.

How Friendship Helps

Friendship, then, helps with your dating relationships. How? Is it that important to build a friendship with someone and create a solid foundation? It is! Here's why.

Friendship builds common ground

If you take the time to become friends, you're building a bridge between two people. Call it the Bridge of Compromise. In the course of your friendship, you'll meet on that bridge often. You'll realize that you don't always have to have your way, and that realization is vital in dating relationships. If you share a history and common ground under that bridge, then you'll approach things together. You'll be a team.

Friendship creates a bond

In addition to building common ground, friendship creates a bond between you and your friend. When you hurt, your friend hurts. When your friend is depressed, you're depressed. When your friend is happy, you're happy. Building a friendship together creates something that's stronger than a mere dating relationship. Through working together, hanging out, and sharing experiences, you'll make a friend for life.

Friendship builds for the future

Whether the two of you have planned to date forever, or just to spend your sophomore year together, or just to take life as it comes, you're developing something for your future. And that something may not always include dating. You're getting to know someone who will be a lifelong friend.

The more you include other people in your relationship, the more support and encouragement you'll have when your life together gets rough.

Friendship includes others

As you build a friendship, you're building other people into your relationship. The more you include other people in your relationship, the more support and encouragement you'll have when your life together gets rough.

When you've got common ground with someone, when you've

created a bond with them, and when you include other people in the friendship, you're ensuring that your relationship will be as healthy as it can be, and you're building a strong relationship that will last.

The Three "Factors"

What should you look for in a friend who's a potential date? How do you build a friendship with someone you're interested in dating? It's not an exact science, but there are things to look for in a friend who might become a potential date. These three factors solidify a friendship with a current friend and build a friendship with someone you'd like to date. Here's each of the three with a short description and questions to help you apply them.

The "In-Common" Factor

The "in-common" factor is simple. This friend or potential friend you'd like to date ought to have something in common with you. Do you like the same things? Do the same things make both of you mad? The two of you ought to at least agree about and have several things in common.

Maybe you've already got someone in mind whom you'd like to go out with. Maybe you already know that the two of you have things in common. Sometimes, though, it's not easy to spot the things you have in common. It's not easy to know who you might have more in common with. So use the questions below to help you sort out the things you have in common with a friend.

Think of several opposite sex friends. For each friend, answer these questions.

- In general, what do you have in common with this person?
- What things do you enjoy doing together?
- What things do you not have in common with this person?
- Evaluate: Do you have more things in common with this person or with someone else?
- Evaluate: Which is weightier—the things you have in common or the things you don't have in common?

The Time Factor

If you're going to date a friend, the two of you ought to have spent some time together—a lot more than you might think—more than just walking home together or going to the movies. And, look. This is time *together*—not on the phone and not chatting on the Internet. You can't get to know someone just by talking on the phone, and you'll never really know someone you've just IMed for a year. The "time factor" means that you're together . . . physically in the same place.

How do you and your friend get good time together? Plan for times when you can be together. Going to the movies or renting a video doesn't count, because you're probably not talking or getting to know each other. Knowing how much time or what kind of time to spend together takes some thinking and planning. Use the questions below to help you decide how much time you need to spend with a potential date.

Think of several opposite sex friends. For each friend, answer these questions:
- Do you enjoy spending time with this person? Do you look forward to being with him or her?
- What could you do with that person that you'd enjoy, and would be "quality time"?
- What could you do with this person that would help you know more about him or her?
- Evaluate: Which of the friends you're thinking about would you love spending the most time with?

The Talk Factor

Along with spending time with the person you'd like to date, you've got to talk about stuff. It doesn't matter what, but it should *not* be stuff like, "I think you're hot" or "I love the way you play basketball" followed by long stares, sighs, and thoughts about how cute you'll look going to the prom together. You've got to talk—really talk.

To make that happen, ask this person things that will get him or her thinking and sharing those thoughts. They could be about God or stuff that you know the person likes. Use the questions below to help you get started.

Think of several opposite sex friends. For each friend, answer these questions.

- What kind of conversation do you have with this person? Is it active, good conversation?
- What things do you two talk about? Surface stuff, or do you get really deep?
- Can you talk to this person about your spiritual life? Does this person talk to you about his or her spiritual life?
- Evaluate: Which of the people you're thinking about do you have the best conversation with?

Reality Check

Right now you might be thinking, "Okay . . . I know Jenny. She's hot," or "I know Paul. He's cute." You think, "We're good friends, we're gonna go out," or "We get along okay. I'm gonna start dropping hints."

But wait—it doesn't work that way. Just because you're friends doesn't mean you should go out. It doesn't mean that you're made for each other. Yeah, friendship is a great foundation, but it's not a free pass to ask someone for a date, and friendship doesn't make every dating relationship work.

Before you go out with a friend, do a reality check.

Don't have expectations. Here's how it often goes. You meet someone who's really cute and you want to go out with him or her. You build a friendship and from there you expect the relationship to go further. That's not fair to the other person. Friendship means that neither friend has expectations. Friendship means that you're there for your friend, that you walk with him or her in happy and sad times and don't expect anything (like a date with you) in return.

There's no need to rush the dating thing.

Don't take things for granted. Friends can sometimes say or do things that a date can't. So because someone you're going to date is a friend, you might expect to take some things for granted. That might be true, but not always. A good rule of thumb is, on a first date with a friend, act like you would act on any first date. It's best not to feel free to hold your date's hand or anything else physical. Remember, friendship is a great place to begin a dating relationship, but it's not a key that immediately unlocks the door to other, more intimate acts.

Don't rush it. When you're hanging out with someone of the opposite sex who you really get along with (and who obviously loves being with you) the tendency is to push the relationship thing. When two friends "like" each other, they both feel the urge to push the relationship to the next step. If/when you're in this kind of situation, remember: there's no reason to rush it. If you're good friends, you'll be together no matter what. There's no need to rush the dating thing. Continue hanging out, keep being friends, and let the next step of your relationship develop naturally.

Friendship. You've got to have it. For any good, solid dating relationship, first you've got to be your date's friend. Then, you've got to have a healthy respect for the other person. How do you build respect into a relationship? What do you do when someone doesn't respect you? Respecting your date is essential, and the next chapter will help you learn how to do that. Keep reading.

➡ Connecting with Yourself

- Make a list of your friends who are of the opposite sex. Write down what you appreciate about each friendship.

➡ Connecting with Your Friends

- Ask your three closest friends what they think makes a strong friendship. Talk with your friends about what it's like to date a close friend. Is it safe? Does it work out well? What elements of dating a friend make it a little weird?

→ Connecting with Your Parents

- Ask your parents to tell you what they think is the foundation of a healthy relationship.

→ Connecting with God

- Ask God to help you form strong friendships with people of both sexes. Ask God to help you develop friendships with potential dates.

Six

The Truth About Respect

When Jim and Sarah began dating they got along really great. But after about six months, Jim began to resent Sarah's belief about driving within the speed limit. Now when they get into the car to head out on a date, the verbal battle begins. Sarah wants to drive because Jim always drives too fast. She believes it's dangerous and wrong to break the speed limit. Jim hates the way Sarah drives. He feels she drives too slowly and that it takes her forever to get anywhere.

Honor and respect—two essentials in every dating relationship.

The difference in their belief about obeying the speed limit has gotten under Jim's skin, and it's gotten ugly. Beyond arguing about who will drive, Jim gets nasty with Sarah and uses the speed limit argument to pick on some of Sarah's weaknesses. The argument isn't just about driving, it's about her bad driving, and how stupid she is, or how slowly she does everything.

And the argument might not have anything to do with Sarah. If Jim's had a bad day, he'll pick at Sarah. His picking usually starts a verbal battle and someone ends up with hurt feelings.

Jim has a problem honoring and respecting Sarah. If he respected her, he wouldn't make fun of her driving. If Jim honored Sarah, he wouldn't let his bad mood motivate him to verbally wreck her.

Honor and respect—two essentials in every dating relationship. Before we leap into the whole idea of how we honor and respect each other in dating relationships, take a sec and jump into the Bible with me. You may be asking yourself, *Why should we honor each other? Why is it important to respect your date?* The answers to those questions are found in God's Word.

Remember the passage from Genesis we talked about a few chapters ago? Remember God's words when he finished creating humans? He said, "It is very good." Think about that. God could have created humans any way that he wanted. He could have slapped a few molecules together, stepped back and said, "Well . . . I could do better, but this is *okay*. It's good enough." No, God created us, looked at what he had done, and said, "It is very good."

What do those words mean for us? The Bible specifically says that we're created in God's image, and that we're *very good* creations. That means we need to treat others like they are God's very good creations, and we should expect to be treated like we are God's very good creations. In fact, Scripture is loaded with passages, comments, and statements by God about how much worth we have. We are valuable to him—so valuable, so loved that he sent his Son to die for us.

You have worth. You have potential. You are loved by the God who *chooses* to love you. That fact ought to rock you. Among other things, it screams how much value you have. When people try to tell you you're nothing, God thinks you're everything. When people treat you like dirt, God waits to comfort you. Each of us is a creation and a reflection of God. You should treat his creation like God's very best work. And you should expect to be treated like God's very best work.

For a variety of reasons, some people make a habit of dishonoring and disrespecting their dates. Other people seem to enjoy being treated with dishonor and a lack of respect. Who are these people? Here are four examples.

The Dude Who Wants to Rule His Date

When Jenny first met Todd, he was the kind of guy any girl would want to take home to her mom. Todd was good looking and, better than that, he treated Jenny well. He opened doors, he helped her with her chair, and he spoke kindly to her. He was the best.

About three months into the relationship, Todd changed just a bit. When Jenny wanted to go out with her friends, Todd seemed agitated and wanted to know where she was going. Todd grew more and more possessive, bugging her about where she was going, until Jenny finally stopped going out with her friends. It was easier to hang out just with Todd and avoid the hassle.

Guys like Todd don't want a relationship with someone; they want girls they can be in charge of.

But Todd still wasn't happy. When they went out, he felt like she was eyeing other guys, wanting to go out with them. Todd decided that he and Jenny ought to just watch movies at one of their houses. After he got her to accept that, Todd went to work on the way Jenny dressed, asking her to wear more modest clothing. Once Jenny changed the way she dressed, Todd went to work on how often Jenny was allowed to talk to her friends at school. Eventually, everyone lost track of Jenny.

Guys like Todd don't want a relationship with someone; they want girls they can be in charge of. Guys, do you feel a need to rule over your girlfriends? Do you feel that you've got the right to be her master? That's not treating her like she's God's very good creation. It's not honoring and respecting her. Don't rule her. She's not yours to rule.

And girls, do you think you're always supposed to be submissive to guys, and that guys (being the men) are supposed to be in charge of girls? Be aware that many guys with low self-esteem or feelings of insecurity will act out by dominating their girlfriends.

The Girl Who Wants to Be Her Date's Slave

Leslie has loved Ben since before they started dating. Leslie, in fact, has had a crush on Ben since they were kids. Growing up in the same neighborhood and going to the same elementary school, Leslie and Ben often played together. They often met after school and after homework would goof off until dinner.

When they started dating, Ben began to see a side of Leslie he hadn't seen before. Leslie would often speak badly about herself and even degrade herself. When she made simple mistakes, she'd often respond by saying, "There goes stupid Leslie again." When Ben came over to watch television, Leslie went out of her way to serve him. Yeah, you're supposed to be kind to guests, but Leslie would often go too far. She'd often bug Ben, asking him if he wanted anything to eat or drink. She'd ask to massage his feet. It was as if she were created to serve Ben, and she'd do anything (including degrading herself) to serve him.

Any relationship that diminishes the other person—makes him or her feel like a lesser human—denies that person's value as God's very good creation.

It's one thing to be respectful of a guest or be kind to someone. It's another thing to think of yourself as someone's slave. Don't think that I'm pushing a twenty-second-century idea of dating where women dominate men. But many sub-cultures in America still teach girls that they're supposed to serve men all the time. And to prove that women ought to serve men, these cultures often use Bible passages about women being silent or serving men.

And let's be honest guys—we love being served, don't we? We love having someone bring us big beefy sandwiches with cold drinks. When we're done, we love to have someone vacuum us off, wipe our mouths, and then go to whip up a dessert. Many of us guys will actually seek out a girl who's willing to serve us at her own expense.

But that kind of relationship doesn't honor the girl and it doesn't honor God. Any relationship that diminishes the other person—makes him or her feel like a lesser human—denies that person's value as God's very good creation.

Girls, do you let guys treat you like slaves? Do you act like slaves because you think you're supposed to? That's not the reason God created you. It's not honoring yourself—you, who are God's very good creation. And it doesn't honor God. Remember, you are the very reflection of God himself.

The Guy Who Hopes His Date Hates Him

Pete acts like an idiot. No one has to tell him how worthless he is—Pete is more than happy to verbally demean himself about how stupid or clumsy he is. And Pete has a talent for finding people who love to make fun of him, who will nitpick at all his quirks. And if no one picks on him, Pete picks on himself—"Yeah, stupid here keeps making mistakes"—just enough to annoy everyone, just enough for everyone to feel sorry for him. If someone tries to be nice to Pete, he shrugs it off and says, "I don't deserve anyone being kind to me."

People like Pete are difficult to respect, because they don't respect themselves. They serve as willing punching bags because they think they're not worthy to be honored and respected. And because people like Pete can't accept honor and respect, there's little chance they can give honor or respect to someone else.

The Girl Who Thinks Her Date Is Trash

Beth hates guys. She *hates* them. No joke. No one knows why. When Beth and her friend Lindsey get together, Lindsey usually has a few good things to say about the "lesser of the species."

Not Beth.

So when Beth began going out with Matt, everyone was amazed. And Beth and Matt's relationship is probably what you'd expect. Beth introduces Matt to her friends as "The Idiot" (she says it with a smile).

She constantly orders him around, and tells him in front of others how stupid he is. Matt doesn't seem fazed by Beth's comments and, in fact, seems to like them. Each time Beth slams on him, Matt smiles or shrugs.

God's design for any relationship—marriage, dating, or just friendship—is mutual respect.

These relationships help you understand how dishonoring your date happens, and how your date might expect to be dishonored. Both girls and guys can hate the opposite sex. Both girls and guys can turn themselves into slaves for their dates. Both sexes can want to dominate a relationship or want someone who'll be dominating. Both can think they don't deserve to be treated well. But God's design for any relationship—marriage, dating, or just friendship—is mutual respect. You can't think you're superior to your date or that you were made to be a doormat. Neither one is healthy.

None of the relationships described above are healthy. The people in the examples either have a problem giving respect or they don't think they're worthy of any respect. What these people need isn't a date. They need others to come alongside them, and walk with them, and help them understand that they are God's very good creations. If any of those situations describe your relationships, you're not being respected, and you don't understand how valuable you are to God.

If You're Not Being Honored or Respected

All of this talk about honor and respect makes you realize that we don't live in a perfect world. If we're talking about how important it is to honor a date, we're doing that because so many dating couples *don't* honor each other. Each year hundreds of couples self-destruct because someone in the relationship chooses to dishonor his or her dating partner.

How do you know if you're in a dishonoring relationship? Ask yourself the following questions:

Do I feel dishonored? Simply asking yourself that question makes you think about how much your date is actually honoring you. It's totally possible for you to get comfortable with being treated poorly and not notice it. Are you being respected in your dating relationship? If you have trouble answering, ask a friend who honors and respects you to answer that question for you about your current relationship.

Am I afraid? Sometimes when we allow someone to treat us poorly for too long, fear grows and we don't feel like we can make a healthy decision on our own. Are you afraid of your date? Is there anything your date does that causes you to question your emotional, spiritual, or physical safety?

Am I Being Treated Like God's Child? Truth is, the heart of every good relationship is God, and a God-centered relationship reminds both people of God's love. Love motivates both people to treat each other like they're God's children. Are you being treated like that? If you can't answer that question with a huge *yes* then you might want to rethink your dating relationship.

If you're in a relationship where you're being dishonored, get out. You don't have to ask permission of the other person, and you don't need to stay in the relationship and hope the other person changes. When your date doesn't respect you, when he or she treats you like dirt—get out. Explain to that person the value that you have and tell him or her that you don't feel you're being respected.

How to Honor and Respect Your Date

Respecting and honoring your date can seem difficult. It's sometimes tough to be patient with what your date believes, how he or she does things, or what your date wants to do with his or her life.

So how *do* you honor and respect your date? First, realize that the person you date is not exactly like you. You two don't look the same. You don't act the same. You have different values. You probably have different goals. So begin by honoring and respecting those differences. Second, realize that your date is, in many ways, a lot like you.

**Always imagine that God is present with you on every
date, and act like he's there.**

How do you begin learning how to honor your date? Here are a few
ways:

Your date is God's awesome creation. Treat him or her like it.

Earlier we mentioned that because each person is created in God's
image each person has value and worth. Always imagine that God is
present with you on every date, and *act* like he's there. Treat your date
like he or she has worth. Demonstrate to your date that he or she has
value. Be polite. Listen to what your date has to say. Talk to your date
like he or she is an important person. Don't make fun of your date, or
the things he or she says, or the way your date acts.

Your date is someone's child. Treat him or her like it.

Your date is someone's kid. Your date has parents. Someone once
changed your date's diapers, helped him or her learn to walk, and saw
him or her off to the first day of school. Your date's parents have worked
hard to shape their child into the person that he or she is.

When you go out with your date, his or her parents are at home,
hoping and praying that their kid has a good, safe time. You don't
need to get neurotic and second-guess everything you do, but you do
need to consider how your date's parents might respond to the way
you're treating their child.

Your date has parents. Talk to them.

You've seen your date's parents standing at the door. You've heard
them talking in the background when you call. Have you met them?
Your date has parents that love and care for him or her beyond your
imagination. Your date's parents want to get to know you. They want
to know what you value, and they want to know what you're like.

So instead of ignoring your date's parents, talk to them. When you call, and your date's mom or dad answers, talk to that parent. Ask how he or she is doing. Tell your date's parents about yourself. Ask if you can have a date at their house, eat dinner with them, and spend time getting to know them.

Your date has feelings. Respect them.

When you go out with someone, you've got a long list of things to remember: keep your manners together, don't eat like a slob. With so much to remember, it's easy to forget that your date has feelings, and emotions, and thoughts that are exclusive from yours. How do you show your date that you respect what he or she thinks?

Listen to your date. When your date tells you what he or she thinks about the food you're eating, or the movie you just watched, or the idea you just spewed out, listen. After you've listened to your date, respond with something that shows you were listening. When you listen to your date, you're demonstrating that you respect the person and what he or she has to say.

Your date has a purpose in life. Help him or her with it.

It's not your responsibility to make sure that your date fulfills God's call on his or her life. But your conversation with your date ought to at least enhance his or her pursuit of it. You can ask your date questions that help him or her think more about how God is calling, or you can help your date pursue what God is leading him or her to do.

This isn't the kind of thing you do in the first few dates. After you've hung out with your date for a while, helping your date hone his or her call is the kind of thing a good friend, and a good date, would do.

Your date has a body. It's his or hers. Leave it alone.

Your date's body is their own property. Inappropriate touching might not be a concern on the first few dates, but after you get comfortable around each other, it gets easier to give in to the temptation. When you touch your date inappropriately you're showing your date that you don't respect him or her. Your actions are showing your date that you expect a physical response to the relationship you've started.

Honor and respect your date beyond his or her own imagination.

You can't honor your date if you're touching him or her inappropriately, or using your date's body to fulfill your sexual desires. If you're tempted to touch your date, don't. If you've already begun to dishonor your date by touching him or her, stop, and explain why you're not touching him or her anymore.

Honor and respect are hugely important, so honor and respect your date beyond his or her own imagination. Treat your date like he or she ought to be treated, multiply that by ten, and go beyond your date's wildest dreams.

Let's say you're going out with someone. Maybe it's a first date for you, and you want to put the stuff from this chapter into practice. How do you do that? The next chapter gives you some tips before you set out on that first date.

→ Connecting with Yourself

- Write out a commitment to yourself, stating that you'll not allow yourself to treat a date poorly or be treated poorly by a date.

→ Connecting with Your Friends

- Make an agreement with a friend, stating that you'll talk to each other if either of you feels like a date has dishonored you or that you have dishonored a date.

→ Connecting with Your Parents

- Ask your parents how they expect you and your date to treat each other. What level of honor and respect do they want you and your date to have for each other? Ask your parents to regularly remind you of their expectations.

→ Connecting with God

- Ask God to help you honor and respect the person you're currently dating, and to help you recognize if you're treating a date poorly.

Seven

The Truth About the First Date

Aww *M-o-o-o-m,* you think. *Why are you wearing that flowered shirt? Why do you insist on embarrassing me?*

What's worse than going on a first date? Going on a first date with your mom as the driver. Now you're standing at your date's front door and your mom is back at the car, waving you on. Wearing the shirt. The world's most embarrassing shirt.

You could just not ring the doorbell. You could *act* like you rung it, *act* like your date didn't answer, and not be embarrassed. You could save your date the embarrassment of riding in the backseat with your mom as the chauffeur, listening to your mom's stories about when you were young. You could save your date from your mom's flowered shirt, too.

What do you do?

A first date isn't easy. It can be scary, exciting, nerve-racking, and fun all at the same time. First dates have the reputation of being tense. You and your date can't possibly learn everything about each other, but one of you might learn enough to decide you don't want a second date. You're on your toes and on your guard all evening. But there are ways to ease into that first date experience and help you have a good time while remaining calm, cool, and collected.

How to Ask Someone Out on a Date

At an earlier time in history, it was customary for the guy to do the asking and the girl to do the waiting. These days, however, who asks first depends upon your family, your date's family, and what the two of you feel comfortable with.

**"I've got time this weekend. Want to get a pizza
and talk? I'll pay you."**

How do you ask someone on a date? Take this test.

1. You're standing in the lunch line. You've wanted to ask her out since last year. You've planned. You've decided . . . you're going to ask. What should you do?
   A. Say, "Hey sugar. You. Me. The movies."
   B. Say, "You're probably already busy this weekend, so I won't ask if you want to go out."
   C. Do an exotic dance, try and impress her with your moves. Maybe she'll go out with you.

2. He's been on your mind all day. You're not sure how he'll react to you asking him out for pizza, but you can't resist. You catch up to him on the way to the school parking lot. What should you do?
   A. Say, "Ben, I love you. Let's have pizza."
   B. Say, "I've got time this weekend. Want to get a pizza and talk? I'll pay you."
   C. Give him a picture of your mother, then say, "This is me in twenty years. Interested?"

Are any of those options realistic? Are any of those options things you might do or say to get a date? Probably not. Wouldn't it be great if there were a list of the perfect ways to ask someone out? The truth is, there's no magic formula for asking someone to go on a date. Need some easy-to-remember ideas for asking someone out? Remember these three basic principles of asking someone out.

Be honest. If you're going to ask someone out, then ask. Don't beat around the bush. Be up front with what you want to ask, and don't annoy the person by dancing around the question.

Be specific. Don't ask someone to go out "sometime." Ask the person to go to a specific thing. Say, "There's a dance next Friday night. Would you like to go together?" If you're specific the person will feel better about the date and you'll have your first date plan set.

Be willing to accept rejection. If you ask someone out, and that person says no—accept it. Don't be a baby or sulk about it. The individual you asked out isn't saying that you're a bad person; he or she is just declining to go out with you.

Need more advice? Great. Here are two categories of ideas that will help you: *basic first date philosophy*, and *putting on your game face*.

Basic First Date Philosophy

Check with your parents. The most important thing you can do before you go out with someone is to let that person meet your parents. Give your parents a chance to meet your potential date *before* you go out with that person. And be sure to ask your parents for their dating advice. They'll probably have some kind of story about how they asked someone out or how they got asked out. Your parents are probably a great, unending, massive pool of dating information. They've already dated, they've already been on a first date, they've already made themselves look silly for the sake of the opposite sex. They probably have some advice for you about how to ask someone out or what to do on the first date. But beware. Introducing your date to your parents can cause ripples. Let's say that you're a girl, and a guy asks you out. You introduce him to your mom and she loves him. Later on, the guy turns out to be a real geek. You'll have to face your mom's endless questions about the guy and why you don't go out with him again. If your parents end up liking someone who's a real creep (or if they can't stand the person), be honest with them about how you feel and be sure to listen to their input (and follow it, if they tell you to steer clear of someone they don't like).

Consider yourself. Think, *How would I want to be asked out?* Approach your potential date the way you'd like to be approached. Think, "What would I like to hear from someone who's asking me out?"

Get personal. We'll cover this more fully later, but it's important to say one thing here: Get comfortable talking face-to-face to the opposite sex. Not over the phone. Not in an Instant Messenger conversation. Not yelling from across the parking lot. There's no reason to be nervous about talking to the opposite sex. Imagine that you're talking to someone you know well. Once you're comfortable talking with members of the opposite sex, you're ready to take the next step and ask someone out. Asking someone out over the phone is like sticking your toe in the water to test the temperature. Asking in person shows a huge amount of respect. Yeah, you can call someone up if you want (and if you're a chicken), but face-to-face is better.

Putting on Your Game Face

Beyond philosophy, and beyond feelings and emotions, you can do practical things to get yourself together before you ask someone out on a first date.

Believe in yourself. Self-confidence is attractive and makes others want to know you. There's a difference, however, between self-confidence and arrogance. Arrogance is the absence of others on your mind, and self-confidence is the absence of your self-consciousness on your mind. When you're not thinking about how self-conscious you feel, you're more focused on others and on the good you can do for them. Before you ask someone out, or before you get asked out, you've got to believe in yourself. You can't walk around, hanging your head, staring at your shoes. Believe that no matter what the other person says about you, their opinion can't change who you are and who God created you to be.

Smile! Especially when you see the person who you want to date. Smiling more will help your mood anyway, and it's good for you. So whether or not you see the person you're trying to attract, you're still doing something nice for yourself.

Be yourself, and learn to be comfortable with who you are.

Make yourself visible. Does the person you want to go out with play a sport? Go to that person's games. Does he or she play in band? Go to that person's concerts. Does he or she participate in drama? Go to that person's plays, and be sure to compliment him or her afterward on his or her performance. Showing up where your prospective date is will increase your visibility and also get you involved in that person's interests. Doing that will give you something to talk about while you're getting to know each other!

Be presentable. There's nothing wrong with trying to look a certain way that *you* like. Just be careful about trying to look a certain way to impress someone. If you're a sporty, casual girl and you like a guy who's into ultra-feminine women, is it right to trade in your basketball shoes for high heels and your jeans for a flowery dress? Nope! Especially if you hate high heels and flowery dresses. Be yourself, and learn to be comfortable with who you are. If you like the way you look, and you feel comfortable in your own skin, don't waste your time with guys or girls who'll only like you if you look a certain way.

Practice! Don't think I'm crazy; practicing how you'll ask the person out is a good idea. Yeah, you're gonna look a little silly for this one, but get comfortable talking to yourself in the mirror. Get comfortable practicing with your best friend. Practice helps you think through what you want to say, it will help curb your nervousness, and it will make you feel more prepared. Practice!

How to Handle Yourself on Your First Date

Want some simple, easy to remember advice for your first date? Calm down! Breathe!

If you've already been on a first date, you probably know that your nerves go nuts. You constantly worry about what the other person thinks of you. You constantly worry if you're doing everything right. You worry that you'll make a huge mistake and make yourself look like a goober. Remember, both of you are nervous. It's okay to be nervous!

With that out of the way, what are some things you ought to do on a first date?

The Do's of a First Date

Be yourself. Your date wants to get to know you, not the alter ego you've assumed for the evening. Be confident about who you are and your date will notice and want to know more. Remember, you're not on a date to perform for someone. You're getting to know someone better and aiming to have a great time.

Smile and be positive. Happiness is contagious, and a sense of humor is a quality that others will notice.

Make it your goal to get to know your date and form a strong friendship.

Listen. Let your date know you're interested in getting to know him or her. Ask your date questions about himself or herself. And remember that body language communicates just as much, if not more, about how you really feel. Look your date in the eye. Lean forward as he or she talks. Let your face and your posture communicate that you are interested in what your date is saying.

Have fun. You're not getting together to solve all the world's problems or to pick your life mate. Relax and enjoy the company you're with. Try not to worry about every single word you say or every little thing you do. Make it your goal to get to know your date and form a strong friendship. Those two goals are as far as you can and should go on a first date.

The Don'ts of a First Date

Here's where the honor and respect from the previous chapter come into play.

Don't talk about yourself the whole time. Remember that conversation requires the input of two people. If you talk about yourself throughout the whole date, you're telling your date that all you care about is *you.*

Don't move too fast, too quickly. No one wants to spend a first date evaluating how the relationship is going so far and talking about starting a committed relationship! If you do, you're expecting too much and you'll scare off your date.

Don't flirt with other people. This is the worst thing *ever* to do! When you're out with someone, don't gawk at people of the opposite sex, and don't try and ask someone else out. It's rude. It's mean. You'll just embarrass yourself.

Don't abandon your date if you see your friends. If you see your friends while you're on a date, it's cool to say hi and even introduce them to your date. But don't go off with your friends and leave your date alone and wondering where you are.

Don't talk about other guys or girls you used to like or go out with. No one wants to be compared to someone else. Focus on your date and give that person the respect her or she deserves. Keep the conversation comfortable and enjoyable.

How Do You Know if a Date Is Going Well?

If you're both having fun, that's a sign that your date is going well. Other signs might be that conversation is easy and flows naturally, you have a lot in common and a lot to talk about, and you find yourself smiling throughout the entire evening. If all this happens *and* your date suggests you two go out again, then you've definitely had a successful date!

If you feel like the date is going well but you're not sure about the other person's feelings, you could suggest another date. If your date seems interested, exchange phone numbers and set up another date right there. If you don't feel that bold, consider waiting until the end of the date, see how the thing ends, then decide. But what if your date is really into you and you're not feeling so hot about them? What if your date wants to go out with you again, but you're just not interested?

The most important thing on a first date is don't get too far ahead of yourself.

Be honest! Don't lead your date into thinking that you're interested in going out again. That would be cruel. If your date asks if you want to go out again, consider mentioning the option of being friends. Not every person you go out with will be a good match for you. That doesn't mean you or your date have some terrible flaw, or that you or your date are creepy. It just means you're not a match. Being up front is sometimes hard to do, but it shows that you're mature. Your date might be briefly disappointed, but on the other hand, no one likes to be lied to, and in the long run your date will respect you for your openness.

What if the Date Is Awful?

Let's say you're out on a date with someone and things are going great. Then by the end of the evening your date begins to get pushy about kissing. Before the evening is over, your date is all over you, trying to get you to make out.

If someone is being inappropriate, rude, or asking you to do things that you don't want to, find a way to get out of the situation—immediately. If getting out immediately means you'll have to call your parents from a pay phone or sit in a restaurant and wait for someone to come get you, that's okay. It's better to get out of a dangerous situation and experience a little discomfort than get hurt because you're caught in a bad situation.

If the date is going badly (your date chews with his or her mouth open, smells bad, or tells you that he or she can't stand you) don't freak out. Be polite, stick with the date until it's over. Even if you don't click romantically with the person, perhaps you've made a friend.

When Things Go Too Well

Sometimes a first date can go so well that you feel ready to profess your love at the door as you're saying goodnight. But hold on! After just one date, you don't know a person well enough to decide if you're in love. Think! After one date you don't know if you're ready to spend the rest of your life with a person. You don't know that person well enough even to kiss him or her. You're not ready to pick out furniture, buy a car, or go shopping together for a puppy.

The most important thing on a first date is don't get too far ahead of yourself. Go slowly, and don't jump to conclusions about your date or your relationship. Be realistic about what you see in the other person, and try not to let your emotions get out of hand. When you imagine more than you should, when you give your heart away on the first date, you set yourself up for a disaster.

Be careful. Be cautious. Don't do or say anything that you'll regret later.

After your first date, you might want to leap into the spiritual side of your relationship. If things go well, your mind races. You want to introduce your date to your church friends. You want your youth pastor to meet your date. You feel close enough to have devotions together. Before you allow your mind and your emotions to take over, read the next chapter and learn more about the glue that keeps relationships interesting and connected.

⇒ Connecting with Yourself

- Make a game plan for your first date. Draw up a list of things you want to do and say on your first date.

→ Connecting with Your Friends

- Talk to your friends after your first date. Don't gloat or play up the date, making it more than it really was. Instead, give your friends an honest account of what happened—both good and not so good.

→ Connecting with Your Parents

- Before you actually go out, invite your parents to talk to and get to know the person you're going out with. Ask your parents to give you their opinion about that person.

→ Connecting with God

- Commit your first date to God. Ask him to be glorified in your first date. If you've already begun dating, ask God to be glorified in your entire dating life.

Eight

The Truth About Intimacy

Superglue is amazing! A small tube, a few chemicals, and you can put almost anything back together. I've always wondered, though, who designed the tube that superglue comes in? Superglue tubes have to be pierced at the top before you can use them. When you poke a hole in the metal seal, the glue flows out all over your fingers, gluing your hand to the tube.

I'll bet the same people who designed the tube designed the cap that comes on the tube. After you once use the glue, the superglue glues the cap to the top of the tube. So the next time you yank the cap off the tube, glue comes out and, again, sticks the tube of glue to your hand.

Yup. Superglue is pretty sticky stuff. And relationships are held together with something even more durable. It's called intimacy. Don't let the word or the concept scare you. Intimacy can help you have a great dating relationship. But it can also leave you with a mess on your hands. It all depends on how close you get and how quickly you get close.

Defining Intimacy

It's inevitable—if you go out with the opposite sex, you're eventually going to connect with someone. You might not be able to imagine actually connecting with the opposite sex, but it'll happen. The more you hang out with that person and the more you get along with each other, the more you'll feel like you're connecting.

That connection is perfectly natural. God created us to have a strong connection to the opposite sex, and when two people of the opposite sex get together that natural, God-created connection will begin to form. Those feelings of connection are often called intimacy.

Intimacy falls into three categories: emotional intimacy, physical intimacy, and spiritual intimacy. Intimate acts include such things as kissing, holding hands, sharing deep feelings, and even praying together.

No doubt you're asking yourself, *Who cares?* Intimacy sounds awfully boring, doesn't it? But it feels nice to be deeply, emotionally connected to someone you're interested in. It feels great, too, to be physically connected to that person. It's natural to want a spiritual connection as well.

But you have to be careful about how intimate you get with a date. Intimacy is easy to mess up. The more you connect physically, emotionally, or spiritually, the more connected you want to become. When intimacy forms on a low level—like holding hands, sharing your dreams for the future, or praying together before a date—it's safe. If intimacy goes deeper than that, you're in dangerous territory. When any of the three kinds of intimacy is pushed past where God intends them to be, you can hurt yourself and the person you're dating.

To help you understand the three kinds of intimacy, here's some information that, as you date, will help you to honor God, the person you're dating, and yourself.

Emotional Intimacy

Emotional intimacy often has many levels. Lower levels of emotional intimacy are shared between casual friends or between people who date. Deeper levels of emotional intimacy are shared between married people.

Emotional intimacy is formed through spending time with another person, and it grows over time and through different situations. Each time you hang out with your friends, you're creating a level of emotional intimacy. That emotional intimacy is the glue that holds you and your friends together through good times and bad.

That same glue is formed when you hang out with someone of the opposite sex. The more time you spent with the person you're dating, the more that glue binds the two of you together. The more emotional glue, the closer and tighter the bond.

The emotional glue that God intends for you to have with someone of the opposite sex isn't intended to exist in all of your dating relationships.

Deep emotional intimacy, however, is designed to be experienced between committed people who have a deep, emotional connection. Parents and their children, family members, and married couples all are supposed to experience deep emotional intimacy.

Deep, emotional intimacy, however, isn't supposed to be experienced between young dating couples. Emotional intimacy is easy to create, and it's easy to mistake your relationship as being ready for deep emotional intimacy. Because we often use married couples, or couples that have been dating a long time, as our examples for how to date, we often think that we should be experiencing the same level of emotional intimacy that they have.

But remember—the emotional glue that God intends for you to have with someone of the opposite sex isn't intended to exist in all of your dating relationships. And it won't exist one week into a relationship. The deep emotional connection that you are designed to have with your date is built over time and through sharing experiences together.

Emotional intimacy is created too quickly (and in a very unhealthy way) when either of the two people in a dating relationship comes from an emotionally unhealthy home. When one or both people come from emotionally dysfunctional homes (either because of emotionally unhealthy parents or because of abuse) the emotional bond between dating couples can get unstable. One person or the other in the relationship gets too committed too quickly and expects the other person to be equally committed (and is offended when they're not). Or one person or the other is overly committed some days, and on other days couldn't care less about the relationship.

Remember—the world doesn't revolve around the person you're dating.

When you're involved in a relationship that's too emotionally connected you need to get out and get some distance between you and your date. You need to reestablish who you are and reconnect with your friends and the people who love you. You also need to encourage the other person in your relationship to reconnect with his or her world and possibly get counseling.

So how do you hang out with someone you "like" and guarantee that your emotional intimacy won't get too deep too quickly? Here are some guidelines:

Recognize your real world. Emotional intimacy goes too far when you exclude your friends and hang out only with the person you're dating. Emotional intimacy goes too far when you rely too much on the person you're dating. Remember—the world doesn't revolve around the person you're dating. That person is only one human being, and your world needs to be bigger than that one person. You're an individual apart from the person you're dating, and it's unhealthy to forget your friends and family.

Include other people. To prevent emotional intimacy from getting too deep, include others in your relationship. Invite other people to go out with you on dates. When you hang out with other people or couples, be sure to include everyone in activities and conversations.

Don't always be together. When you first start dating someone, you're *always* with him or her. Here's an idea—don't spend all of your time with that one person. Time apart will make you look forward to being together and make you more enjoy your time with him or her. Make room for time with your friends and let the emotional connection with your date grow slowly.

Physical Intimacy

Physical intimacy isn't limited to sex. Physical intimacy includes simple touching, such as knowing someone well enough to touch or hug that person. Like emotional intimacy, physical intimacy has many levels, and ranges from a simple handshake to sex.

Any touching outside of holding hands is an inappropriate step toward physical intimacy. Girls, if he says he wants to give you a back rub because you look stressed out—say no. Guys, if she says she wants to sit on your lap and cuddle while you watch a movie—don't let her. Physical intimacy was created and designed to be experienced within the context of marriage. Any physical touch either of you initiates erodes the awesome gift that is waiting for you when you get married. Physical intimacy will be covered in more detail in the next chapter, so hang tight and keep reading.

Spiritual Intimacy

Spiritual intimacy is experienced by people who share a common religious belief. And, like emotional and physical intimacy, spiritual intimacy has many levels. Believers who meet for worship share a low level of spiritual intimacy; married couples often share (or ought to share) a deep level of spiritual intimacy.

Spiritual intimacy is intimacy at the deepest level.

So every believing dating couple will be spiritually intimate—to a certain extent. But as your relationship with your date progresses, you may want to pray together or study the Bible together.

Here's a caution, though. Don't rush into becoming spiritually intimate with your date. Just as rushing physical intimacy can hurt you and the person you're dating, rushing spiritual intimacy can also hurt you. That's because spiritual intimacy is deeper than the emotional intimacy you experience with your date, and goes beyond even physical intimacy. Spiritual intimacy is intimacy at the deepest level. That's why spiritual intimacy is to be handled carefully.

The Purpose of Couple Devotions

Scripture is loaded with examples of people who had incredibly intimate moments with God. Jesus, before he's arrested, cries out to God in the Garden of Gethsemane. Moses, while tending sheep, is called by God, and God touches his spirit. Paul, on his way to kill Christians, encounters God and experiences the most holy moment of his life.

These examples don't show how unmarried couples are supposed to handle themselves in God's presence. But they do help us understand how humanity has interacted with God and how God has interacted with his creation. Through watching God and Moses interact, through listening to Jesus' prayer in the Garden, we realize that we can and should reach out to God through prayer and through reading his Word.

These moments are recorded, too, so we can also understand another thing—humanity has access to God. We don't have to stand far away from him, we don't have to hide anything from him, and we can have a personal relationship with him.

The purpose of a quiet time with God is for personal devotions, which help us to grow in our relationship with our Creator. It's a chance to confess our sin to him, ask him to direct our future, and to reveal things about ourselves that he wants us to change. The quiet times we spend in personal devotions, connecting with God, are therefore deeply intimate.

Many things happen during your quiet time with God. You open a very personal side of yourself to God. As you confess sin, you ask for help about important issues. As you ask him to guide your future, you're inviting him to direct everything you do. In your quiet times with God, you open every possible thing inside of you that is completely personal. Those moments impact your past, your present, and your future. Your personal devotions touch, in fact, the very heart of who you are.

Married couples share a deep level of commitment to each other. And because of that commitment, they share emotional and physical intimacy at the deepest level. Married couples, then, share the most personal parts of themselves. So they are ready to share all those things that are revealed to God during their quiet times with him.

Couple devotions between unmarried people form an unhealthy connection between two individuals who have not covenanted together before God in marriage.

Sharing your personal devotion time with someone you're not married to means sharing the most personal things about yourself that you share only with God. If you have couple devotions with someone you're only dating, you too quickly create a deep bond with the other person. More important and more damaging, you also express things to God in another person's presence, things that are too personal and too private to be shared in a dating situation.

The spiritual bond that often forms when couples have regular devotions together isn't, then, appropriate outside of marriage. Couple devotions between unmarried people form an unhealthy connection between two individuals who have not covenanted together before God in marriage. When this bond is formed, the level of intimacy, the level of self revelation, is deeper and more intimate than you may be ready for.

Healthy Alternatives

You don't need to have personal devotions together to be a Christian couple. You don't need to have personal devotions together to show others that you're a serious Christian couple. It doesn't impress God, and it isn't the magic formula that will help your relationship be stronger. But there are healthy alternatives.

Worship together. If you and the person you date attend the same church, and it's okay with your parents, consider sitting together during worship times. Sitting with your date during church gives you the chance to worship God in the presence of the person you're dating. It gives both of you a way to grow spiritually at the same time.

Group Bible studies. If your youth group offers Bible studies, try attending together. If only one of you attends a Bible study, consider inviting the other person to go with you. This is another chance for you to grow spiritually, and it offers the two of you opportunities to talk often about spiritual things.

Semi-regular prayer. It's not okay for unmarried couples to get together *regularly* for prayer or Bible study. Now and then, however, it's okay for couples who have been dating a long time to share prayer requests with each other, pray together, or read Scripture.

Study topics. If you feel very strongly that you want to study the Bible together, consider reading and researching together some topics where both of you can learn and contribute. Studies on specific important biblical concepts like love, sin, or the church are excellent ways to study God's Word together.

Spiritual and emotional intimacy aren't the only dangerous areas you need to keep your eye on. Physical intimacy and the desire to show affection are huge temptations and can make us do stupid things. Is displaying affection okay? What kinds of displays of affection are acceptable? How much touching is okay? There's help for you in the next chapter. Keep reading, and discover how to show healthy affection for your date.

→ Connecting with Yourself

- If you haven't already done so, establish a regular pattern of quiet times. Include Bible reading and prayer every day.

→ Connecting with Your Friends

- Talk with your friends about when they think it's okay to get close spiritually, and when it's okay to pray together or study the Bible on a date. Ask your friends if they've ever struggled with being too emotionally close in a relationship.

→ Connecting with Your Parents

- Ask your parents what they think about you and your date having devotions together. Discuss the idea of spiritual dating with your parents and together come up with an understanding that you're comfortable with. If you're in a relationship ask your parents to help you evaluate if you're too emotionally connected with your date.

→ Connecting with God

- Ask God to help you and your date maintain a healthy level of intimacy, and to keep your relationship fully devoted to him.

Nine

The Truth About Affection

Here's a quick quiz. Take it and see how you do.

1. Jason and Kelly are on their first date. It's been an awesome time. Jason has walked Kelly to her front door, and he's leaning in for the big kiss good night. Kelly's mind fills with all kinds of reactions. She's not sure if she should kiss him. The date's been good, but she's not sure that it's been *that* good. What should she do?

   A. Let him kiss her good night.

   B. Offer him her cheek.

2. Sarah and Ben have been going out for forever. When they get together, things seem really cool. During the times they're alone and the times when they kiss, things feel like they ought to progress. Lately, Sarah's been commenting that she'd like to take the physical side of their relationship a bit farther. What should Ben do?

   A. Allow the relationship to progress physically.

   B. Keep his hands to himself.

3. Steve has been all hands since the first date. Even though he's way too forward, Missy just can't get enough of his personality and his sense of humor. On top of that, Steve is really great

looking. Lately, he's been more forward with his touching, and Missy feels like she wants to give in. She likes the way Steve makes her feel, and she'd like to feel it some more. What should she do?

A. Give in, and let him touch her more.

B. Stand her ground, and tell him to keep his hands off.

What kind of affection is okay with your date?

---

4. Nick has approached Paul in the locker room. Nick's been after Julie for the longest time. He likes her—he really, really likes her. The problem is, Julie doesn't like him at all. Nick makes things really bad for himself when he hangs on her, tries to hold her hand, and touches her. Julie asks him to stop, but he doesn't get the hint. Now he's telling Paul that he's going to ask Julie out for this weekend. He wants Paul's opinion. What should Paul do?

   A. Tell Nick that he is dishonoring Julie and he should leave her alone.

   B. Encourage Nick to ask Julie out.

Is it cool to touch each other? Is it okay to kiss a lot? How much touching is too much? What kind of affection is okay with your date? It's okay to wonder about what kind of touching is appropriate on any date. You can't get a clear answer from a silly quiz like the one above, and you probably shouldn't rely on a friend to help you understand what appropriate affection is.

Before we dive into this subject, though, let's get one thing straight.

Hormones are racing through your body. Hormones make you do, say, and think crazy things. When you want to touch someone of the opposite sex—that's your hormones working. When you have sexual feelings about someone of the opposite sex—that's your hormones working.

There's nothing wrong with feeling what you're feeling. The effect of the chemicals on your body are part of God's design for you. The tough part about dealing with hormones is *dealing* with hormones. So . . .

- How do you control the way they make you feel?
- How do you keep your hormonal feelings in check?
- How do you disobey what they're urging you to do and instead follow God's ideal?
- How do you keep your hands to yourself?

That's what we're after—keeping our hands and our hormonal urges to ourselves. Because what's important is how you respond to your hormones and the decisions you make (or don't make) as a result of their influence. Let's start with a few definitions.

Healthy Affection

Affection is when you show someone that you care. When you give a guy a CD of your favorite songs, that's an affectionate gesture. When you give a girl a rose, that's an affectionate gesture. Affection can be a good thing.

Healthy affection is stuff that's not going to harm you or the person you're dating. Healthy affection seeks to build up the person you're dating. Healthy affection would *never* lead you to touch your date in an inappropriate way. Healthy affection combines the principles of healthy touch with godly respect.

Unhealthy Affection

Unhealthy affection is anything that's disrespectful, that is emotionally or spiritually harmful, and that goes against what God says about how you should act. It's the opposite of healthy affection.

Certain kinds of affection can seem okay, can feel pretty good, and can be rationalized—but still be wrong. And here's where your hormones can help you learn about self-control. There's nothing easy, magical, or enjoyable about saying no, but that's exactly what you have to say to yourself (and to the person you're with) when your affection has passed a point and become sexual. Learning this lesson can be frustrating, and people often just don't get it until it's too late. But the truth is, the more you give away now, the less you have to give to your spouse. It may sound stupid now—when giving in to your hormones is something you'd really, really like to do—but later on you'll regret it, when you realize your spouse was not your first. Then, that first moment of weakness will matter.

So if this is such an important subject, does God's Word say anything about healthy affection? Truth is, God's Word doesn't say, "Couples, don't kiss" or "Never touch each other." God's Word does, however, give us excellent guidance for how we should treat each other and how we should think about each other. Check out Philippians 4:8–9:

> Finally, brothers, whatever is true, whatever is noble, whatever is right, whatever is pure, whatever is lovely, whatever is admirable—if anything is excellent or praiseworthy—think about such things. Whatever you have learned or received or heard from me, or seen in me—put it into practice. And the God of peace will be with you.

You want to know what kinds of affection are okay? Interested in learning about what kind of touching is cool? What's appropriate to think about? Philippians says to think only about things that are admirable, praiseworthy, and excellent.

Want to practice the kind of affection this passage describes? Then commit your affection to behavior that is only praiseworthy. Work to make everything that you do right, pure, lovely, and admirable. And encourage it in the person you're dating, as well.

The Big Smooch Fest

Let's just say it—kissing rocks. Kissing is loads of fun. The huge problem with kissing is that it's so difficult to just kiss.

Think of kissing as the beginning of a roller coaster ride. Imagine being strapped into the seat of a coaster, but instead of the ride being controlled by some guy who's employed by the amusement park, you've got control. With the ride ahead of you and the controls in front of you, you've got a series of choices to make. How fast will you go? What direction will you turn? How many loops will you take? With the car in your control, you can go as fast as you want.

Let's just say it—kissing rocks.

That's the kind of control you have over kissing. You can go fast, you can go slow. You have the ability to take your kissing in a variety of directions. Remember—the decision to do anything physical (kissing, inappropriate touching) involves two people. Any physical mistakes you make won't just hurt you, they'll hurt the other person too. Remember—*you* are in control. Not someone else. Not a dude at the controls of the ride. You. And kissing can be the beginning of a really, really bad ride. Kissing can get you started on the road to inappropriate sexual behavior. So you've got some choices to make.

Be careful with kissing. The decision to kiss and how often to kiss is totally up to you and your date. You don't have to kiss each other at all. You can choose to leave everything physical about your relationship to another moment. You can wait to kiss until your relationship becomes more serious and kissing is a commitment both of you want to make. However you choose to kiss, remember to be careful with how much you choose to do it.

Make specific plans. Always plan for something to do on your dates. If you're alone together one evening with nothing planned, sitting on the couch kissing, you're headed for trouble. Don't put yourself in that situation. Go out together to places where you're not completely alone and tempted to mess around.

Not in Public!

When you've allowed your affection for each other to be displayed by kissing, it can become too easy to kiss in public, holds hands, put your arms around each other. When you do that, it's called PDA (public display of affection).

If you're hanging all over your boyfriend or girlfriend and being sloppy all over each other in public, you need to know something. People are watching you. They're making fun of how you and your date constantly touch each other. They're talking about how it's gross that the two of you kiss in front of everyone. They're commenting about how weird they feel when you hang all over each other. So I've got a little message for you PDAers from your friends:

Stop it!

When you're hanging all over each other in public, it signals a lot of things. First, it signals that you're likely willing to be even touchier in private. Second, it signals your disrespect to the person you're with. It makes them look "loose" and trashy.

If you're careful . . . the way you express your feelings for each other can be an awesome, godly profession of your healthy relationship.

When you allow your affection to mutate into PDA, you need to ask yourself, "Have I become too comfortable in displaying my affection? Have I gone too far?"

Issues For Your Parents and You

Healthy affection. PDA. Kissing. There's a huge list of stuff to be constantly thinking about. But affection isn't really a time bomb. If you're careful, and if you're honest, and if you're realistic with your date, the way you express your feelings for each other can be an awesome, godly profession of your healthy relationship.

But if you allow your chemicals to rule you, and allow your affection to go nuts (expressing itself in *huge* make-out times, hanging all over each other, pawing each other), then you're definitely headed for trouble. When it comes to issues of healthy affection, you should be talking to your parents.

It's an awesome and amazing thing that young people are waging a battle not to give in, and are waiting until marriage.

Talk with your parents about the gray areas of affection. Whether or not to kiss, have long make-out times, hold hands, put your arms around each other—these are issues that your parents have opinions about. If you haven't already talked to them about the boundaries they'd like you to date within, do that now.

Talk with your parents about sex. Go ahead, do it. Walk up to your mom or dad and say, "So. Let's talk about sex." After your mom or dad freaks out, they'll likely want to talk with you. Your mom or dad will probably talk about what sex is and help you with ideas to avoid allowing your relationship to get sexual.

Talk with your parents about your body. The hormones that are pushing you to make unhealthy choices with affection are biological. Ask your parents about them. Your mom and dad have been where you are. They've struggled with the whole affection and hormone thing. They probably have advice about how you can control yourself.

Sex—Saying No in a Yes, Yes, Yes World

Sex is everywhere. It sells products, it's connected with music, and it's offered as a solution to loneliness. In this sex-saturated society, many students are choosing to remain virgins. It's an awesome and amazing thing that young people are waging a battle not to give in, and are waiting until marriage. Not everyone is doing *it*.

There's a lot you can do to stay sexually pure.

When impurity isn't cluttering your mind, you're less likely to give in to temptation.

Stick close to God. God often does a wonderful thing. He puts us into situations where we have no choice but to rely upon him for strength. By doing your best to stay close to God, you're creating a bond with him that will give you strength to stand up for yourself. Make it a top priority to spend time every day reading your Bible and praying. You don't have to live like a monk or be a spiritual giant. Just give some time to God every day. Staying focused on God's Word and God's voice will keep you close to him so you can tap into his strength.

Avoid sex-filled stuff. Don't rent R-rated movies. Don't watch explicit music videos. Don't look at sexually explicit magazine pictures. Avoid Internet pornography. If you keep impure images out of your life, your mind stays pure. When impurity isn't cluttering your mind, you're less likely to give in to temptation.

Be accountable. Have someone in your life, besides God, whom you have to answer to for your actions. Find a friend who understands the struggle of staying sexually pure. Meet with that friend once a week for Bible study and prayer and to talk about how you're doing with staying sexually pure. Neither you nor your friend has to have all the answers. Just help each other, supporting and praying for each other. This person should be the same sex as you and be someone you trust and know really well.

Your Big Picture

When you start to get serious in a dating relationship, developing strong emotional feelings for someone, it can be difficult to keep your perspective. Remember how kissing can be like a roller coaster? Well, we often get on that coaster, the ride starts, and we lose our perspective. We fail to remember that we have our entire life ahead of us, and we forget that we're making choices that will impact our entire future. In other words, our willingness to give in to our hormones and emotions causes us to lose sight of the big picture of our lives.

The desire to give in to your affections constantly pushes you to take your eyes off that big picture. Desire demands that you focus on and obey your immediate urges. So here's a three-step challenge. Read each of these steps, and consider how you might answer each one.

Step One

This first step is crucial, and it's about accomplishments. Think of what you want your life to look like. Imagine how you'll feel five years from now when you remember how you're living right now. What would you want to remember about yourself? What do you want to have accomplished in the next five years? How will giving in to your hormones prevent you from accomplishing that? How will it mess up your plans? How will it distort your memory of who you were at this age?

Take this first step by doing this:

- Take an honest look at your life. What do you want to do? What do you want to accomplish?

The best way to deal with temptation is be honest about it.

Step Two

This second step involves thinking realistically about how you're feeling and what you're experiencing. We're all tempted differently, our bodies react differently to our sexuality, and we each feel differently about that temptation. It's easier, though, to ignore that temptation or give in to it than to be honest about it. But the best way to deal with temptation is be honest about it.

Get honest about temptation by doing this:

- Think realistically about the direction in which your body might be pulling you. How are you tempted? How are you feeling about being tempted?

Step Three

Finally, after you've thought realistically about what you want to accomplish, and after you've been honest about temptation, think about concrete steps you can use to avoid giving in to temptation. Feel free to use any of the information you've read in this chapter to answer the following question.

- Think concretely about how you can avoid giving in to your urges. What are some specific things you can do or say when you feel like giving in to temptation?

Look. As a teenager, you have a lot on your plate. Schoolwork, extracurricular stuff, family things. You need a release. You need something new and interesting to do. Your body is urging you to use your feelings of affection for your date to release your tension. But you need to keep your eyes on your big picture. Recognize how easy it is to lose sight of what God wants you to accomplish. Make a conscious decision not to give in to your chemicals.

What fuels the desire to move into unhealthy affection? Love? Feeling like you're in love? When you're convinced that you're in love, you're more willing to give in to your desires. What is love? How do you know if you're in love? Keep reading, and you'll discover what real love is.

→ Connecting with Yourself

- Talk to the person you're dating. Together, make some decisions about what physical boundaries you'll put on your relationship.

→ Connecting with Your Friends

- Discuss with a friend the smart choices you can make about the physical side of your dating relationship.

→ Connecting with Your Parents

- Talk to your parents about your sexual feelings and desires. Ask them to help you avoid making wrong choices.

→ Connecting with God

- Ask God to help you make healthy decisions about your affection. Ask God to help you honor your date by not touching him or her, or dishonoring your date's body in any way.

Ten

The Truth About Love

Ahhh, love. Is it the feeling you get when the person you want to go out with passes and your heart skips a beat? Is it the way he makes you feel when he assists in the game-winning touchdown? Is it how you feel when she tells you that there's a piece of lettuce stuck in your teeth? Love is one of the most difficult words to describe. Below check any of the boxes that give an accurate definition of how you'd describe or define love.

❏ Forgiving	❏ Frightening
❏ Patient	❏ Sex
❏ Honest	❏ Dividing
❏ Blunt	❏ Difficult
❏ Dangerous	❏ Useless
❏ Cuddly	❏ Mysterious
❏ Painful	❏ Real
❏ Serious	❏ Complex
❏ Comfortable	❏ Slow Dancing
❏ Familiar	❏ Life Changing
❏ A Stranger	❏ Confusing
❏ Unusual	❏ Pizza

Yup. Love is difficult to define. Everyone is looking for love of some kind. Children who are raised without love end up living stilted lives, constantly searching for meaning. People who have loveless lives often fill the void with empty, short-term relationships, and with alcohol, drugs, and other things that lead to a dead end.

You can define and describe love in a variety of ways, and understand it based on how you were raised. Here's what I mean. Read through the following different ways people understand and perceive love.

Will: Will was never held as a child. His parents left him in his crib all day, dropped in a bottle every now and then, put a television in his room. Will's parents never interacted with him. When Will grew up, all he wanted was to be held. For Will, being held is the ultimate act of love.

Perception: Love equals physical touch.

Mary: Every time Mary's dad said he loved her, it was either in the midst of verbal abuse or just after he'd hit her. Mary's mom never intervened and usually let her dad rule the house with anger and abuse. As an adult, Mary associates love with abuse. Every time Mary meets a guy, she expects to be hit or sworn at.

Perception: Love is physical abuse.

Understanding what love is begins with how God defines love.

Sam: Sam's parents spent as much time as they could with him. When he was a baby, Sam's parents held him, took pictures of him, made baby noises at him. Sam's parents did everything they could to raise what they thought would be a "healthy child." As a result, Sam expects the love he experienced as a child to be reflected in his relationships.

Perception: Love is healthy, caring, and fulfilling.

Will, Mary, and Sam perceive love in different ways, so they define love in different ways. Usually love is defined based upon how we're raised. If you're raised in an unhealthy situation, there's a chance you'll live out that unhealthy definition of love. If you're raised in a healthy, loving home you'll likely live out that healthy definition of love. However you were raised, you'll expect that same kind of love from your dating relationships. Many of us need to learn and relearn what love really is. Understanding what love is begins with how God defines love.

Biblical Definitions of Love

The Bible is God's love letter to us, describing his love for each of us. That's why love is everywhere in the Bible. God's Word in the original Greek language contains three unique and distinct concepts of what love is and what love can be. Each word translates into "love" in English, but in the original Greek means something entirely different.

Agape: *Agape* is unselfish, unconditional love. *Agape* seeks the best for the other person, and continues to love that person no matter what he or she does. A perfect example of *agape* is the way God loves us, and the love that Jesus displayed for us on the cross. This kind of love should be an element in every relationship, whether with family members, friends, or people you date. *Agape* shows maturity in your relationships and focuses on the needs of the other person rather than on your own needs.

Phileo: *Phileo* is friendship. We feel *phileo* toward people we have fun with and enjoy spending time with. *Phileo* is not exclusive to a dating relationship—you can feel *phileo* for a friend, a teacher, a relative, or anyone close to you.

Eros: *Eros* is sexual love. *Eros* in a marriage relationship is an expression of the love that a husband and wife have for each other. A marriage cannot stand on *eros* alone, but combined with *agape* and *phileo* is part of a happy marriage. The expression of *eros* requires a marriage relationship, and should never be acted out between unmarried couples.

When the word *love* is used in the Bible, it most likely refers to *agape, phileo,* or *eros.* Your Bible, though, doesn't use the words *agape, phileo,* or *eros*—it uses the word *love* to encompass their concepts or meanings. These three concepts of love aren't merely ones that the Bible has chosen to highlight; they're the three basic elements of love within the human heart.

Look again at those three different biblical concepts of love. Have you ever felt a kind of love other than *agape, phileo,* or *eros?* Probably not. Those elements of love are part of the human psyche, included in the way God created us.

God intends that you feel *agape, phileo,* or *eros* in different amounts, for different people, at different times in your life, and for different reasons. But it's not always easy to identify which element of love we're feeling, and in what amount. That's the challenge of *agape, phileo,* and *eros*—identifying them and giving each the right amount of weight, so that we honor God as we love each other.

The Great Love Struggle

It can be tough in any relationship to give the right amount of weight to *agape, phileo,* and *eros.* You probably already know how easy it is to go overboard, giving a lot of weight to *eros.* It's easy to feel *eros* for the opposite sex, and easy to give in to those feelings. But it's also easy to give a lot of weight to *phileo,* pouring all of your emotions into your date in the name of *phileo,* and surrendering (for the sake of your love) your entire social life to your date. When we don't understand what love is or how it operates in our psyches, we can easily give everything we have, everything we are, and every area of our lives over to "someone we love."

Agape. Eros. Phileo. When you combine all three of these, you get an incredible picture of surrender. But think about it—depending upon the situation, complete surrender can be a healthy concept or an unhealthy one.

Every good relationship that's risen to the level of marriage ought to contain *agape, phileo,* and *eros.* Your dating life, however, shouldn't have all three in the same proportions as in marriage, and you shouldn't act on *eros.* Marriage is made complete with the combination of *agape, phileo,* and *eros.* But dating relationships that act on *eros* mess up God's plan for you.

Love and Your Heart

Your heart is where you feel loved and where you're motivated to respond lovingly. Your heart often rules your body, and sometimes you can't control how your heart will pull you. But when you express authentic, godly love through your heart, you can do some really great things—both for your date and for others in general. That expression turns your love into something awesome.

Your date and you ought to be selflessly seeking the absolute best for each other.

Others-oriented. When real, godly love is expressed through your heart, you become a person who seeks the success of others and who lives selflessly. You'll want the absolute best for the other person. It was this godly love from the heart that led Jesus to the cross.

How does this others-orientation seep into your dating life? Your date and you ought to be selflessly seeking the absolute best for each other.

Strong. Godly love expressed through the heart creates an unbelievably strong love. This love is solid—you can smack it with your fists, squeeze it, drop it off a building. It won't break. Real, godly love is committed, lasting through trials and struggles, the good and the bad times. How does strong love figure into your dating life? If your love is real, it will last through bad moments.

More than a feeling. Without godly love, your love is just emotion—a feeling. But godly love expressed through the human heart creates a love that is much more than feeling. This kind of love motivates to action. It moves people to do and say things that they wouldn't ordinarily do. It moves you to act when you don't feel like acting, to love the other person when they seem unlovable.

How does this more-than-a-feeling love help your dating life? You'll love your date when they're in a bad mood. Your date will love you when you don't look your best. Your love will be more than just emotion.

Love and Your Head

Your head is where you rationally approach relationships and where you decide to love in healthy ways. When it comes to expressing godly love, no one knows which acts first or strongest—the head or the heart. It likely depends upon the person and the situation. But a head that expresses godly love thinks differently than a mind that expresses purely human love.

Loving thoughts. When godly love is expressed through your mind, you think good things about others. Unhealthy mental images aren't present, and you don't think about things that might hurt others.

Loving thoughts are needed in your relationship. Why? If you're thinking loving thoughts about your date, you're not thinking lustfully. You're not plotting a way to get your date alone so you can act on your lustful thoughts. When real, godly love is expressed through your mind, it helps you love your date with your mind.

Even though we know God, and even though we're trying to date the right way, the way we form relationships and the way we understand love can get mixed up.

Loving decisions. When godly love is expressed through your mind, the decisions you make will be healthy and loving. Those decisions affect others and affect you in positive ways. Making godly, loving decisions means that the things you and your date do together will be healthy. Your actions (directed by your decisions) will enhance your relationship.

The Love Confusion

In a dating relationship, not all decisions, actions, and feelings are loving. Even though we know God, and even though we're trying to date the right way, the way we form relationships and the way we understand love can get mixed up. When we get love confused with other emotions and behaviors, all kinds of problems can result. Here are three major areas where we get love confused.

What do you do when you're convinced that love exists, but the other person doesn't know you're alive?

You're invisible. Ever been there? You've fallen for someone and you can't get that person out of your mind. You think about the person when you're eating spinach. You have the person on your brain when you're getting a tooth filled. You're *sure* you're in love, and you're convinced that the person knows how much in love the two of you are. So when you talk to that person about your combined future, you're amazed that he or she didn't know you existed.

What happened? What do you do when you're convinced that love exists, but the other person doesn't know you're alive? Honestly, you're not feeling love, you're feeling a deep sense of "like," and it happens to *everyone*. If you feel this, don't attack the other person. Help that person get to know you, and let him or her see how cool you are. Maybe something will develop.

"I'll love you if . . ." Sometimes being loved comes with conditions. Your date might say something like, "I'd love you more if you'd go with me to the game." Your date might not even actually say it but hint that your relationship would be better if you'd do what he or she asks. This conditional love isn't real love. If a person says that he or she will love you if you do something, that person will only love you if you keep doing those things. The "I'll love you if" line is conditional love, and it is distorted. If your date uses it, get out of the relationship.

"I love only you!" Ever been in a relationship where you can't get away from each other—and you don't want to be away from each other? The feeling that you can't be apart is a dangerous side of a relationship, which isn't healthy love. Yeah, it's okay to want to be together a lot, but when you're never apart, you end up creating a small world that excludes friends and family. That's not good! If you're stuck in an "I love only you" relationship, you need to broaden your world, hang with your friends and family, and give your date a few days away from you.

How do you know if your love glorifies God?

The Love Quiz

It can be difficult to know how to have a healthy love relationship with your date. *Eros, phileo,* and *agape* can be confusing. It's easy to get them mixed up, and it's hard to know which one you're feeling, or which one someone may be feeling for you. How can you know if you're in love? How can you know if your love is healthy? How do you know if your love glorifies God?

There are no simple, short answers to knowing if you're in love. But here are ten questions you can ask yourself to evaluate if you're really in love and if the love you're feeling is healthy and godly.

1. Is your date's love godly? Is yours?

We can learn about love from being loved by God. God's love for you is immense, unending, radical, profound, and beautiful. His love is everlasting, and he draws us to him with "loving-kindness." Does your date's love seem godly? Does yours? Is your love for each other fueled by your strong connection to God?

2. Is there trust between you?

It's tough to find someone who's trustworthy. When you do, it's okay to want to hang on to that person and want to date him or her. So ask yourself, "Does the person I'm dating exude faithfulness? Is he or she trustworthy? Am I trustworthy?" It takes a mature person to be faithful. Are you that mature? Is your date?

3. Does your date have ulterior motives? Do you?

Remember Judas' famous kiss of betrayal? Jesus and Judas were friends, and Jesus trusted Judas—until he knew about Judas' plan to betray him. Although Judas walked the walk of a disciple, he was also walking the walk of a betrayer. He said he loved Jesus, but his actions spoke otherwise, because Judas had ulterior motives. The dating kind of love can be the same. Your date might say, "I love you," but he or she might also do or say things that speak otherwise. Maybe your date acts in ways that make you feel like he or she doesn't love you. Maybe your date says things about you that are unloving. If so, your date may have ulterior motives, and having ulterior motives in a relationship isn't loving. Does your date seem to have ulterior motives? Do you?

4. Are you and your date witnesses?

Everyone will know the One you follow by how you treat your date. Everyone will know the One your date believes in by the way he or she treats you. Sure, this guideline could be apply to strangers, your family, and friends. But it could easily apply to the people you date. Actions speak loudly about a person's belief in God. People are watching you and your date to see what you believe and how much you believe it. How you and your date treat each other doesn't necessarily reflect how real your love is. It does reflect how healthy your love is. If your love is healthy and pure, your relationship will be a strong witness for Christ.

A relationship is more than physical attraction.

5. Is your date helping you be your best? Are you helping your date be his or her best?

A new command I give you: Love one another. As I have loved you, so you must love one another. By this all men will know that you are my disciples, if you love one another.

John 13:34–35

This verse means you ought to do your best to help your date be his or her best. In a strong relationship both people help each other be the best that each can be. As someone who cares about your date, you should encourage that person, comfort him or her, and urge that person to live a life that honors God. Do you? Does your date?

6. Does your date try to confuse you? Do you try to confuse your date?

Do you or your date try to confuse each other? This might not seem important, but if you or your date tries to confuse each other about your relationship or the importance of purity, you're not being godly. When you and your date discuss issues, are you both willing to look at things from the other's point of view? If not, you or your date are trying to confuse the other person, unwilling to be flexible in your thinking to honor the other person's perspective. When a date confuses you, you're less able to focus upon God, which interrupts your relationship with God. And that's a huge problem. Do your or your date do or say things that are emotionally or mentally confusing? Do you or your date's actions prevent either of you from focusing completely on God?

7. Does your date help you avoid sin? Do you help your date avoid sin?

Even in the best relationships, one person sometimes encourages the other to do bad things. So here's a simple question: Do you or your date encourage each other to go against God's plan for you? Do your or your date encourage each other to go against your parents' rules?

8. Do you feel comfortable to be yourself?

Love often causes us to feel things that seem out of our control—including how we feel about ourselves. Healthy love will cause us to feel comfortable with who we are, so comfortable that we grow more to be who God wants us to be. Love causes us to feel okay about ourselves, and it causes us to help others feel good about themselves. Does your date help you feel your best? Do you want your date to feel his or her best about himself or herself?

9. Is your relationship based upon more than physical affection or physical attraction?

Authentic love is not just an emotion, and it's stronger than the physical attraction you feel for the person you're dating. Yes, it's easy to form a relationship based only on how the other person looks or how that person makes you feel. But a relationship is more than physical attraction. Do you like your date for more than they way he or she looks or dresses? Do you like your date for more than the way he or she makes you feel?

10. Do you enjoy being with the other person?

When some couples first start dating they have loads of fun. Months later the fun dies down and the couple discovers they can't stand being around each other. Although neither person enjoys the dating relationship, they continue to date each other. Although there's no fun, they stick together. You should enjoy being with the person you're dating, and you should enjoy the relationship. Do you? If you do that's another indication that you could be in love.

The ten questions above will help you to evaluate whether you're in love. And don't keep the questions to yourself. Ask the person you're dating the same questions and see how that person answers them. You might want to answer the questions together and then talk about how each of you responded to the questions. If you uncover any areas where you don't agree or find an area where you realize your relationship isn't loving, you might talk with your parents and ask them to help you work out a solution.

This chapter has talked about *agape, phileo,* and *eros,* and it has given you questions to help evaluate if you're in love. A mosaic should now begin to form in your mind about what real love is and about how real love is lived out in a dating relationship. Definitions and quizzes aren't *really* necessary in defining love, but they do help you understand how huge and complex love can be. So remember these ideas about love:

- Healthy, godly, authentic love is a love that seeks to imitate God's love in every way. If you know God and you know what his love is like, you'll probably know whether what you're experiencing is love, and whether or not it's from God.
- Emotions often rule our hearts and minds, creating feelings of love. When these feelings take over, especially when the feelings are new to us, they can cause us to do silly things. Those things may *seem* loving and fueled by real, godly love that is expressed through the heart and mind, but they're not necessarily loving and godly.
- It's easy to confuse love with other feelings. People are often so desperate to find love, they'll latch on to any emotion that remotely feels like love and declare their undying devotion for someone. But remember—deciding that you're in love isn't a casual thing, like deciding between a chicken sandwich or a hamburger. Decisions about love are serious. Love doesn't happen to everyone, and it seldom happens quickly. Real love doesn't happen often during a person's lifetime.

It's easy, in the name of love, to hurt and be hurt. When you too lightly decide to love, you can seriously damage yourself or the person you're dating. Sometimes when love goes too far, or when it's not healthy, someone gets hurt. What happens when love goes too far? Check out the next chapter.

➡ Connecting with Yourself

- Ask yourself what form of love you most strongly respond to. Physical touch? Kind words? When someone does something nice for you? How might the way you respond to love affect your dating relationships?

→ Connecting with Your Friends

- Talk with your friends about the different biblical concepts for the word *love*. Ask them if they've felt the different kinds of love toward their dates.

→ Connecting with Your Parents

- Ask your parents about when they knew they were in love with each other. Ask them how you might know when you're in love.

→ Connecting with God

- Ask God to help you understand his love before you attempt to understand human love. Before you go on your next serious date, pray that you'll show your date the appropriate kind of love.

Eleven

The Truth About Dangerous Dating

Anything good can be used to cause harm. Even snow.

When I was in college, Mike, a guy on my hall, figured out the perfect prank. Kent lived at the end of the hall, right next to an exterior door. After his last class for the day, he often slept until dinner.

One winter day after a massive snowfall, Mike waited for Kent to get back from his last class. When Mike was sure that Kent was asleep, he brought in buckets of snow and packed them against Kent's door. Mike kept at it until he'd packed snow about a foot thick, covering the entire door. Since Kent's room was next to an exit, Mike opened that door to let the winter air in so the snow wouldn't melt quickly.

Love, taken outside the three biblical concepts of agape, phileo, and eros, can be hurtful and actually destroy people.

Kent slept a little late that day. In fact, he slept almost all the way through dinner. So when he woke up and saw the time, Kent knew he had to rush to dinner or starve. He got up, threw on some clothes, jerked open his door—and plowed into Mike's wall of snow. Kent wasn't happy. He was cold, and he was hungry—and he totally lost it.

Kent stalked up and down the hall, yelling and demanding to know who built the wall. Eventually, he calmed down, Mike apologized, and we all had a laugh. A really, really good laugh.

Anything good can be used to cause hurt. Snow, packed hard, can deliver a nasty bump on the head. Love, taken outside the three biblical concepts of *agape, phileo,* and *eros,* can be hurtful and actually destroy people. Love can be good and innocent. But when it's tainted or dysfunctional, it can become abusive.

Not sure what that kind of abuse looks like? Below are a few situations. Can you figure out whether or not they're abusive?

Holly and Jake

Holly and Jake are at the movies. During the movie, Jake puts his hand where it doesn't belong. Holly is annoyed and pushes him away. Then on the way home, Jake tries it again. Holly pushes him away again and asks him to stop. Finally, as they're saying good night, Holly feels his hand, steps back, and explains that he is being inappropriate.

"Holly," Jake responds, "You love me, right?"

"Yeah, Jake, I love you."

"Well then, this is what people do when they're in love. They kiss and do other things. If you love me, you'll want to touch me, and you'll want me to touch you. If we're in love then being physical is okay."

Holly is perplexed. On one hand, she knows that any kind of touching is wrong. But she loves Jake, and she wants him to know how much she loves him.

Before she can respond, Jake says, "Look, Holly. Lots of girls would be happy to express their love in the same way I do. If you're going to be a prude then I can just move on and find someone who'll do what I want."

Holly is confused and doesn't know what to do.

These two are struggling over the issue of giving up your body to someone you're not married to—even if you're in love. Is Jake using love as a means to convince Holly to surrender to his desires? If Holly loves him, should she give in? Take a moment and think through the advice you'd give to Holly and Jake.

Sam and Amy

Sam is speechless. He can't believe Amy decided to do this in front of his friends.

Rewind.

When they began dating, Sam and Amy were just like any couple. They went out with friends, and they seemed to get along really well. After a while, they spent less and less time with others. When they did hang out with their friends, Sam didn't talk too much. When he did talk, Sam spoke in short sentences and was usually interrupted by Amy. When she interrupted Sam, her comments usually began with an angry look at Sam or a comment that demeaned him in some way.

Now, Sam is standing around with his friends. Amy is railing him, saying things he'd hoped his friends would never hear.

Sam just stands there, not sure what to do.

"It's your fault," snaps Amy. "Don't tell me you're sorry or that you'll change. I'm angry because of you. You did this. It's your fault."

"What Amy? What did I do?"

"All night, you've been talking down to me. You've been treating me like a child. You've been acting like I'm completely unimportant. You know you're doing it."

Sam wasn't trying to treat her like a child. Actually, he isn't sure why she's angry. He's so confused he's willing to say anything to get her to stop making a scene.

"Alright, Amy. I'm sorry. I'll stop."

Amy just gets angrier. "Stop treating me like a child. Just keep it up Sam. Remember what happened last time?"

Sam just stands there, not sure what to do. After a few tense seconds, Amy slaps Sam. His friends can't believe it. When Sam doesn't respond, she slaps him again. When he fails to respond again, she kicks him. You can tell by Sam's reaction, this isn't the first time she's done this.

Is it okay for Amy to be this angry with Sam? Is it okay for her to act out in this way? Take a moment and think through the advice you'd give to Amy and Sam.

Ray and Carrie

Carrie sits on the end of her bed, biting her nails. When she hears her Instant Messenger beep, she heads to her computer. It's Laura.

LauraBell: hey gurl. you and ray going out tonight?

Gr8Cares411: yeah. gonna rent a movie and go to his house i think.

LauraBell: cool. what movie?

Gr8Cares411: dunno. look laura. if he starts in with that "you must obey me cause i am male" stuff i'm gonna loose it.

LauraBell: is he still doing that?

Gr8Cares411: yeah. it's like just because he's a guy, he thinks that i gotta do everything he says. it's like i have to obey him. he says it's in the Bible.

LauraBell: really? in the Bible?

Gr8Cares411: yeah, that's what he says. he says that the Bible says that all women must obey all men. he gets really annoying with it too. i'm supposed to get him stuff from the fridge when he wants. he makes me sit in the uncomfortable chair whenever we rent a movie. it's real stupid. but, he says it's in the Bible.

LauraBell: weird. well, lemme know how it goes.

Gr8Cares411: will do. pray for me, k?

LauraBell: yeah. sure will! later.

Gr8Cares411: bye.

What do you think? What advice would you offer to Carrie?

The Rules of Love

Spotting abuse in a relationship isn't always easy. Sure, you can some-times tell when one of your friends is being abused by a date—but you can't *always* tell. When someone in a relationship goes too far or love takes a turn for the worse, the change is sometimes subtle and the abuse not easy to detect. Love goes haywire and gets abusive when one person in the relationship abandons the rules of love for the sake of their own rules.

Yeah, love has rules—and when those rules aren't followed, someone gets hurt. What are these rules? When someone says, "I love you," how should that person treat you?

Love goes haywire and gets abusive when one person in the relationship abandons the rules of love for the sake of their own rules.

In 1 Corinthians, God explains his rules for love. They're his guidelines for how love should be lived out by people who call themselves Christians. But they're also the rules for how love should be lived out by everyone. Just because someone doesn't believe in God doesn't mean that these rules don't work or don't apply.

First Corinthians 13:4–7 draws a complete picture of what love is:

> Love is patient, love is kind. It does not envy, it does not boast, it is not proud. It is not rude, it is not self-seeking, it is not easily angered, it keeps no record of wrongs. Love does not delight in evil but rejoices with the truth. It always protects, always trusts, always hopes, always perseveres.

First Corinthians 13 is everyone's favorite chapter on love. And it could have been used in the previous chapter about authentic, godly love. But by looking at the principles in this passage, we can also learn what love isn't. We can learn how love goes from healthy to unhealthy, from godly to ungodly.

Love is not impatient.

What is impatience?
- It's the dude who's been standing in the fast-food line for longer

than he wants. When the cashier steps away from the register one more time, he verbally attacks the entire counter crew.

- It's the parent who yells at his or her kid for dancing while they're picking a movie at the video rental store. When yelling doesn't work, the parent slaps. When slapping doesn't work, the parent continues slapping and calls the kid stupid. When that doesn't work, the parent drops their videos and leaves the store.

- It's the guy who isn't interested in his girlfriend anymore, but doesn't feel like telling her. Instead, he verbally berates her whenever he can—mostly in public.

Love's patience extends beyond the understanding of the human brain, and bends over backward for the sake of the other person.

The Corinthians passage says that love isn't impatient. That means it doesn't attack when it's stressed out. It doesn't seek to destroy when it's been pushed to its limit. Love doesn't hurt others when it's angry. Love's patience extends beyond the understanding of the human brain, and bends over backward for the sake of the other person.

Love isn't unkind.

Love is also kind. Love's kindness extends beyond feeling and emotion, and treats people with consistent respect.

How do you know when love isn't being kind?

- When the person says that he or she loves you but pressures you to do things that are totally against your beliefs, that person is not being kind. That person doesn't love you with the kind of love that God expects.

- When the person says that he or she loves you but speaks poorly to you or about you, that's not being kind.

Love isn't self-seeking.

Can you love someone and seek only your own interests and desires? Nope. But many people seek only what they want, and try to pass it off as love. How do people do that? They hold out love as a means to get what they want: "I will love you only if you meet my needs."

Self-seeking love says, "You must serve me, because my needs are more important than yours" or "I will get your love, and you're lucky to get anything from me." Self-seeking love promotes the "I" part of the relationship and denies that the "you" even exists. And it goes farther, beyond seeking the desires of self. How?

I can't get my needs fully met if your needs are also important. So in order for me to get my needs met, you have to be diminished. Everything about you—your needs and desires—are unimportant. My needs are the only needs that matter.

Self-seeking love is damaging and abusive. It's easy for the abused person to pass off the abuse and say, "But we're supposed to put others first, and deny our own desires for the sake of another person." That's true, but when two people share real, godly love, they have a mutual desire to see each other succeed, wanting each other to be healthy and happy. When one person is intent on seeing only his or her desires met, the relationship becomes damaging and unbiblical.

What does a self-seeking love look like? Does your date consistently forget your needs and serves his or her own? Does your date pressure you to do things that will make him or her happy? Does your date ignore your needs and complain that you never meet his or her needs? That is evidence of a self-seeking love. When the love in a relationship is used by one person to control the other, that is self-seeking. When one person's love allows the other person's controlling behavior to go unchecked, the other person's self-seeking attitude takes over, and your love starts to stink.

Love isn't easily angered.

Ever spill milk at the table? It wasn't your fault. Maybe your sister put the pickles on the other side of your glass, and you knocked it over trying to get into the jar. Ever trip over your feet? Push the door too hard and it marked the wall? Drop your notebook?

When your parents get mad at you because you spilled your milk, that's a reaction to the spill. Anger often looks like a reaction to something, but it isn't always. It's an attitude. When your date gets mad at you for no real reason, that's not a reaction. That's an attitude.

The 1 Corinthians passage above makes the point that love isn't *easily* angered. That's because everyone gets angry. Anger is a natural emotion that God gave us. But God gave us anger to use at the right time. Unhealthy anger is anger that's easily set in motion, spilling out over some simple blunder. The angry person will react poorly, unleashing anger upon his or her date. The anger will come out as hitting, foul language, snide remarks, and teasing.

Something inside us humans doesn't want just to do wrong things—we also delight in those wrong things.

When anger takes control of someone, that person is incapable of real love. So if your date's anger is at the surface, if he or she verbally attacks you, if your date slaps you, if he or she speaks poorly of you to your friends—that's unhealthy anger. And that's a love you don't need.

Love doesn't delight in evil.

Why does Paul write these words about love not delighting in evil?

It's human nature to do evil things. It goes all the way back to Adam and Eve—they disobeyed God. Since then, humanity has made an art of doing evil things to each other. We start fights, we argue, we do things on purpose to hurt others. And along the way we tell ourselves that doing those things is okay and isn't hurting anyone. And if it is hurting someone, then that person deserves it.

How do we know that people actually think and act this way? Have you ever watched those television court shows? You know the kind—

where two people appear on television, and they have a judge sort out their argument. In almost all of those cases, someone has purposely hurt someone else and justified their wrong actions. Something inside us humans doesn't want just to *do* wrong things—we also *delight* in those wrong things.

How do you know if your date is someone who delights in evil? If you're being treated poorly by a date and that person seems to enjoy treating you badly, that person is delighting in evil. If your date says or does hurtful things to you and doesn't seem to think it's wrong, that's delighting in evil. Paul makes the point that someone who delights in evil isn't acting in love. If your date is doing evil things, he or she isn't acting lovingly toward you.

Why Dating Gets Dangerous

The rules of love are just that—rules. They're like any rules. When the rules aren't followed, the results are not positive, and dating gets dangerous.

Dating gets dangerous because God isn't the focus.

Adam and Eve stopped focusing on what God wanted for them and followed their own desires. Remember what happened to them? Judas stopped obeying Jesus and made a grab for money to betray him. Remember what happened to him? Those two situations paint a picture of what happens when we shift our focus from God to other things. The same thing happens in your dating life. Dating gets dangerous when one or both people in a relationship stop following God's best, and start obeying their own desires.

Remember: Anything without God is messed up, wrong, ends bad, and is totally sinful. So forgetting God causes eruptions in a relationship. When you leave God out of a relationship, refusing to honor him, everything gets out of whack. So if you're in a relationship, you both need to keep your minds and hearts devoted to and focused upon God.

Dating gets dangerous because one of the people is "dysfunctional."

Try to paint a picture of the word *dysfunctional*. What kind of picture do you end up with?

- A guy yelling at his girlfriend in front of her friends
- A guy mentally abusing a girl at dinner
- A girl playing mind-games with her boyfriend so she can get what she wants

Dysfunctional can be defined in a variety of ways. Psychologists and pastors all give a different description and definition. *Dysfunctional* basically means "non-functional," and it's used to explain people or situations that are outside the norm of healthy behavior. Although there are a lot of different explanations about what makes someone dysfunctional, it's often because of a person's family. The dysfunctional person has either been abused by a family member or raised in a difficult home. Things outside the family, like abuse or hurt by a non-family member, can cause someone to be dysfunctional.

Non-functioning persons bring their skewed, unhealthy perspective into a relationship, and they can mess up the people they're dating. How do you know if the person you're dating is dysfunctional? It's not always easy to know, but dysfunctional people are often overly possessive, have unhealthy attachments to people, and constantly work behind the scenes to get what they want.

Dating gets dangerous because selfishness takes over.

Of all the ways sin creeps into a relationship, selfishness is one of the most damaging. You already know what selfishness is, but how does selfishness negatively impact dating relationships?

- A selfish person wants only what he or she wants, never allowing his or her date to choose where they'll eat or what movie they'll watch.
- A selfish person refuses to limit the physical side of the relationship to what his or her date prefers. The selfish person wants to go as far as possible, and what his or her date wants doesn't matter.

Selfish people are the self-seeking people talked about earlier. They don't care about other people, using their dates like tools to bring themselves joy. What the selfish person wants is more important than what his or her date wants.

How do you know when your dating relationship is downright dangerous?

When Dating Gets Dangerous

Selfishness, skewed ideas, and a desire to get physical satisfaction can take over a person's life. When that person doesn't get what he or she wants, that person gets angry. And when that person gets angry, the gloves come off, his or her temper flares, and unhealthy emotional or physical outbursts become acceptable to that person. If you've been the object of an explosive and dangerous outburst from someone who *says* that he or she loves you (but doesn't act like it) then you've been in the trenches and seen the dark part of dating.

It doesn't take a rocket scientist to notice when something in your date has gone wrong. You don't need help to know when you're being abused or hurt. But how do you know when your dating relationship is downright dangerous?

Obsession

Dating gets dangerous when your date can't get enough of you. When he or she has to be around you all the time, has to dress exactly like you, or gets extremely jealous when you talk to anyone else, you're dating someone who's obsessed with you. If your date is mildly obsessed, they may insist that you two dress alike. Signs of more advanced obsession are when your date wants to know where you are all the time and always wants to know whom you're talking to on the phone.

Verbal Abuse

When the person you're dating isn't getting what he or she wants, that person can get nasty. The nastiness usually begins with verbally picking you apart. You know what verbal abuse is, so it's not too hard to spot, right? Not always. Yeah, verbal abuse is swearing at you, yelling at you—things like that. But verbal abuse also takes place when your date picks you apart subtly, letting you know over time how awful or useless you are. Serious and damaging verbal abuse can be quiet and deadly to your personality and self esteem.

Obsession, verbal abuse, and physical abuse are elements that signal a bad relationship.

Obsession plus verbal abuse equals severe emotional abuse. If you're on the receiving end, your psyche can be severely damaged. Who you are—including your personality and your character—can be slammed so much that you become a non-entity in your own eyes. You begin to believe that you're useless, worthless, and completely deserving of any and all abuse that your date lays on you.

Physical Abuse

Physical abuse is a sure sign of a relationship gone wrong. But physical abuse doesn't always leave marks or cause bleeding. Physical abuse is anything that another person does to you that you don't want to happen. Inappropriate touching that you don't want is physical abuse. Light hitting by another when he or she is angry with you is physical abuse. Physical abuse can become sexual abuse when the touching goes too far and moves into forced sexual acts.

Obsession, verbal abuse, and physical abuse are elements that signal a bad relationship. You don't always see them coming, and you're not always sure how to respond. Truth is, everyone experiences one or more of these elements in their relationships—at least to some degree. You can't avoid some rough spots in your dates. What do you do when they happen?

If You're Caught in a Dangerous Situation

When your date behaves or speaks in an inappropriate way, you can't change what happened, but you can change how you react. Remember Kent? After his door was packed with snow, he lost it for a bit. Responding in the right way to something hurtful isn't always easy. It's not always safe to just blow off steam and then go back to the way things were. If you're caught in a relationship you feel is abusive or dangerous, do the following two things.

Get Out!

There's no reason for you to stay in a relationship that hurts you. There's no reason for you to continue a relationship in which you're hurting someone else. No boyfriend or girlfriend is worth your accepting abuse. End the relationship. Explain to the other person that you don't feel comfortable, explain why you're not comfortable, and tell that person that you're breaking things off. It's important to do this somewhere in public, and tell a friend or parents that you're breaking things off. That way if the person attempts to do something more damaging you'll be around people, and your friends will know to check up on you.

Talk to Someone

When you've been hurt, you have to talk to someone. You might not feel like you want to, but you have to. Who do you talk to?

Your Parents

If your date has hurt you, you might feel anxious to talk about it to your parents. Especially if you've also made some incorrect choices with your date. Don't let that stop you from talking to them.

When do you talk to them? If something inappropriate has happened, your parents are the first people you should talk to.

It's true: Anything good can be used to hurt you.

Your friends

Sometimes your friends understand things that your parents don't. Your friends are living life from the same perspective and at the same time that you are. Since they're walking with you through life, they might offer some ideas for getting away from the pain the relationship is causing you or for knowing what to do next.

Your Pastor

After you've talked to your parents, and you've talked with your friends, consider talking with your pastor. Your pastor has a different perspective than your parents or your friends. He can offer you a combination of professional counseling, a biblical perspective, and an objective opinion.

It's true: Anything good can be used to hurt you. That goes for food (eat too much and you get sick), medicine (take too much and you could die), and television (watch too much and you get stupid).

Love, or what you think is love, filtered through unhealthy human perspectives can destroy you. But when love is healthy and grows in good ways, positive things can happen. Sometimes your love for someone can mature in beautiful ways, and you may feel like you're ready for marriage. Are you? How do you know if you're ready for that big step? Keep reading and find out.

➜ Connecting with Yourself

- Examine yourself. Are there elements in your personality that could take a relationship in a dangerous direction? Are there elements in your personality that would tolerate someone taking your relationship in a dangerous direction?

➤ Connecting with Your Friends

- Ask your friends if they've ever experienced a dangerous date. Make a commitment with your friends to talk about any negative dating experiences.

➤ Connecting with Your Parents

- Ask your parents to help you set up standards for the kind of people you'll date. Ask them to keep an eye on the people you date. Ask your parents to talk with each date before you go out for the first time.

➤ Connecting with God

- Ask God to protect you from dangerous dates.

Twelve

The Truth About Making a Life Commitment

The lights are low. The scent of burning candles fills the air. Except for the server, Kim and Terry are alone in the restaurant.

Terry has taken Kim to the most expensive place he can afford. This is the end of an amazing day—pancakes at her favorite breakfast stop, then an entire day at the zoo. Kim was so touched watching Terry at the petting zoo. After a busy morning and afternoon, they both smelled, so they split for a bit to clean up. Terry told Kim to put on her best outfit— seemed he had something special he wanted to ask her.

The last several months have been unbelievable—and now this incredible day. Kim would be willing to repeat it all tomorrow. She's found the guy of her dreams. She's thinking this could be forever— but she's not completely sure.

Terry picks up Kim, takes her to the restaurant, tells her to order whatever she wants. Then . . . he just stares. He looks like a puppy, but Kim thinks it's cute.

Yeah. This is the end of an incredible day. It couldn't be any better.

The questions begin during dessert.

"You love me right?" Terry's always been a little insecure.

He knows I love him, Kim thinks. *He's being silly.* "Of course I love you," says Kim. "You know that . . ."

"You want to be with me forever . . . right? This thing is forever, isn't it?" This question is a bit beyond cute.

"Well . . . yeah. Maybe. I don't know. . . ."

"Look, here's what I think. After high school, we need to get married. I love you . . . I want to be with you forever."

This throws her. After a day like this, and the awesome way Terry's treated Kim, she feels like she owes him some kind of commitment. Does she really want to tell him this is forever . . . forever? The kind of forever where you end up surrendering your free time, friends, and extracurricular activities?

Kim is speechless, so she just stares at Terry. He thinks she's staring because she feels the same way. She's staring because she doesn't want to be honest.

What should she do?

It's the same old story. The guy loves the girl and wants to get married. The girl loves the guy so much that she's ready to commit her entire growing years to being only with him. Isn't that what people do? Fall in love. Spend time together, and then get married. Isn't that the way things are supposed to go?

It's easy to daydream about only the positive moments of married life and never take a real look at marriage as a whole.

This book has covered the subject of love—what love is, what love isn't, how a loving relationship ought to affect you. But this chapter discusses the affect that love can have on your future. Should you marry young? Is it okay to commit to marriage when you're in high school? What's right?

"Marriage?"

Yeah, marriage. And don't lie to yourself. If you've been on a few dates with someone you like, you've played the "what if" game. Guys, you've thought about what it might be like to be married to that person. Girls, you've written your first name with his last name, just to see how it looked. You've daydreamed about being with each other for the rest of your lives.

But many people who've daydreamed about marriage don't think realistically about what marriage means. It's easy to daydream about only the positive moments of married life and never take a real look at marriage as a whole. Take a few minutes and look realistically at the prospect of marriage.

Am I old enough?

Is it okay to get married when you're still a teenager? Should you wait until you're older? What's the right age to get married? Everyone has an opinion about the right age to get married. What's yours? Should you wait until you graduate from high school? Should you wait until you have your college diploma? Is there a "right" age that you should get married? Here's an easy rule of thumb. If you're asking yourself if you're old enough to get married—you're probably *not* old enough.

But you're in love, right? And no one in the history of the human race has felt like you feel. You might not be twenty-five, but your love surpasses your age. The truth is, the right age to get married is between you, your parents, your date, and your date's parents. Outside that small circle, no one else's opinion is relevant.

Think about this, though—as much as you might be in love, you've got your whole life ahead of you. If you're dating someone and feel ready to get married, remember—marriage means attaching yourself to someone for the rest of your life. If you're eighteen or younger, that's a l-o-o-o-ng commitment to make at a young age.

Am I independent?

How independent should someone be before he or she gets married? What defines independence? Some people would say you should have your own house or at least have your own apartment. Others say you should live with your parents until the day you're married. Still others say you should have an income that would support you and another person.

So. what do *you* think about independence? It's a good idea to start thinking about that now. Share your opinion with your parents and other married couples you know, discussing what you think and *why* you think it. Based on what they know now, they probably see things that they wish they had considered.

Am I ready?

Being ready for marriage involves a lot of things—physical readiness, spiritual readiness, emotional readiness. Your parents might want you to wait until you've had more life experience. Others might say, "All you need to know is if you're in love." How do you know you're ready?

How can you know if you're really ready to get married?

If you're older than fifteen, no doubt your body is ready. But is your mind ready? Are you emotionally ready? You're the only person who can really answer that.

Am I being realistic?

It can be tough to be realistic about your emotions and your relationship. Everything in you says that you're completely in love and that you should at least verbally commit the rest of your life to your date. But is committing realistic? How can you know if you're *really* ready to get married? Does knowing depend upon emotions? Does it depend upon your age? Everyone looks for their own signs to help them know if they're ready to get married. A good rule of thumb is to spend some time apart from the person you'd like to marry. Use this time to evaluate your relationship and your readiness for marriage. When you're young and thinking about getting married, many people would like to tell you what they think. If you're lucky enough to have friends who love you and who are willing to give you their opinions, listen to them. Your friends and your parents are the best sources for a reality check. They'll help you sort out how realistic you're being and how realistic you should be.

The Way God Works

Have you ever thought about how you get God's opinion about your life? Has God ever handed you a note from heaven that says, "Tomorrow, at lunch . . . you need to ask this person out for a date."

Nah, he doesn't usually work like that. We usually learn about what God wants for us through talking and listening to other people. It's not like God doesn't want to tell you his thoughts. But often he uses our parents, friends, and pastors to help us learn what he wants for us. That way, God tells us what he wants us to know and gives us someone to hold us accountable for what he has called us to do.

Let's assume that you're seventeen. You've found the person you want to marry. You're ready to give up your life and spend the rest of it with this person. You're sure, but you're not completely sure. What can you do to be sure that you're making the right decision. How can you know that it's okay to surrender your heart?

Use the people that God has placed in your life. He's put them there for a reason, and it's up to you to rely upon them. But keep in mind—when you talk to people, don't expect them to always agree with what you're thinking and feeling.

First, talk to your parents about what you're thinking and feeling. It's okay to tell them where your feelings are leading, that you want to spend the rest of your life with this person. Ask them for their advice and their opinion about the person. If they don't know the person very well, you're in trouble. If your parents freak out and are adamantly against what you're feeling, listen to them.

Second, talk to a lot of other people. Ask your friends—not just the ones that always agree with you. Ask friends who give you honest opinions about what you're thinking and feeling. If they freak out or caution you against acting on what you're feeling, listen to them.

In general, if you're in high school or younger, you shouldn't be thinking about marriage. If you daydream about married life with a person you're dating, realize it's your hormones talking, that it's your desire to rush to adulthood, that it's a case of love unchecked. Sure, opinions vary about whether it's okay to get married while you're still in or just out of high school. But whatever your emotions, if you're thinking about getting married at a young age, rely first on the opinions of your parents and your friends.

My Life Partner

Okay—you've read this far . . . and now you're freaking out. You have no interest in getting married at a young age. You're not thinking at all about getting married. You're not even seriously dating anyone. "Yeah," you say, "I'll give my life to someone—someday. Eventually I'll find someone that I'd like to spend the rest of my life with, and I'll take the plunge."

Deciding who to marry, though, isn't a simple issue like who you'll ask to go to the movies. Marriage is the big stuff. The big kahuna. Marriage means choosing a person to spend the rest of your life with. Because this decision is so important, it won't hurt to start thinking about the kind of person you'd be interested in having as your partner for life. What qualities would you like that person to have?

I'll pick a few categories, and you think through some of your ideas.

Looks

Don't underestimate this category. You might prefer a certain look and only you know what that look is. What kind of physical qualities do you hope your future spouse has?

Spiritual Life

Are you looking for a spiritual giant? Just want someone who has regular quiet times for personal devotions? What kind of person would fit your spiritual makeup?

Personality

What kind of person would best fit your personality? Are you an introvert who's better around extroverts? Do you have a lively sense of humor and would like someone who can laugh with you? What kind of personality traits do you hope for in your spouse?

Occupation

This one's a toughie. Guys, you might prefer your wife to stay home, raise babies, and invest her life in the home. Girls, you might prefer a husband who's a doctor, who'll buy you BMWs, and hand over a few hundred each week just for spending cash. What kind of occupation do you hope your future spouse will have?

You've got your ideas about your ideal future spouse. God has his ideas, too.

Habits

An old saying about newly-married people goes like this: When your spouse leaves the cap off the toothpaste the first few weeks of marriage, it's cute. When your spouse leaves the cap off the toothpaste year after year, it's the most annoying thing possible. Everyone has habits. You have habits, and even your tame habits can get annoying to another person. What habits do you think you could tolerate? What habits do you know would annoy you?

Hobbies

This might be nitpicky, but the hobbies of your potential spouse could be important. What if that person loves woodworking, but you hate sawdust? What if you love raising dogs, but your spouse has pet allergies. What hobbies do you hope your future spouse has?

Assembling the Perfect Person

Okay. You've got your list, and you're prepared to wait for *the* person. What do you do now? There's no easy way to find the person that God has for you, no simple plan for finding or even liking this person. But you can do some things now to help pave the way.

Pray for that special someone. Yeah, right now—ask God to protect your future spouse. Ask him to continue to work on that person,

---

It's not selfish to ask God to prepare you for your future spouse.

---

preparing that person for the time when you two meet and get to know each other. You might feel weird about praying for someone you don't even know yet, but don't let that prevent you from committing to pray for that person.

Pray for yourself. It's not selfish to ask God to prepare you for your future spouse. It's okay to ask God to grow you up, to get you ready physically, emotionally, and spiritually to meet your future spouse. God wants you to ask for his help. He wants to shape you into the perfect match for the person he is preparing for you.

Compare your shopping list. Use the ideas you wrote above to remind you of the unique qualities of the person you're after. Ask a same-sex friend to write his or her ideas for the categories, then trade lists. Note the differences. By looking at another person's list, you can learn a lot about yourself and the kind of person you're looking for.

Be open. You've got your ideas about your ideal future spouse. God has his ideas, too. The person God has chosen for you may not, at first glance, seem your type. So be open to meeting the person he wants you to meet.

Connecting with Yourself

- Read through the list of qualities that you hope your future spouse will have. Draw those and other qualities into a picture, then hang it in your closet. Every time you look at it, remember to pray for your future spouse.

Connecting with Your Friends

- Ask your friends what they want their spouses to be like. You might want to show them your list and compare your ideas with theirs.

→ ## Connecting with Your Parents

- Get each of your parents alone. Ask each what they hoped for in a spouse before they met each other. Ask them to give you advice about your dreams for your spouse.

→ ## Connecting with God

- Ask God to help you be realistic about your goals for your spouse. Ask him to help you be patient while you're waiting for the right person.

Thirteen

The Truth About Dating

Chet was a major hit with women. He had an uncanny ability for getting girls. Within moments of meeting a girl, he knew her name, had her phone number, and usually had set up a date.

When I met a girl I got nervous. Really nervous. I'd never had a successful dating experience, and I was in awe of Chet's ability.

Chet had been dating Laura, who had a roommate named Jacqui who was this tall, extremely good-looking girl. The kind of girl I usually struck out with. The kind of girl I never had any luck with. But I had something going for me. I had a car.

Chet and Laura didn't have cars. So if they wanted to go out, they had to ask me or Jacqui to go along and drive. Chet and Laura didn't want a single tagging along, so they'd ask both Jacqui and me. And we would go . . . as friends.

Through Chet and Laura's dates, I got to know Jacqui, and the more I got to know her, the better friends we became. The more our friendship grew, the more I fell in love. Me—the failure at connecting with the opposite sex—I was falling in love. I didn't know if she suspected anything, and I hoped she didn't. If she couldn't tell I was falling for her, she wouldn't run away screaming, and then maybe I'd have a chance.

What I didn't know was that she was falling for me. The more we hung out, and the closer friends we became, the more we fell for each other.

I can tell you the date we first kissed. I can tell you the exact moment

I knew I wanted to spend all my days with her. I can tell you the date, time, location, and setting when I asked her to marry me. I know exactly what I was feeling and thinking the day we got married. Over ten years later, Jacqui is still my best friend.

Keeping God at the center of your dating relationships is essential.

I was so inept at dating. I was completely insecure. I had no idea how to properly treat a girl. I wasn't sure how to tell her that I loved her. It's amazing that Jacqui and I found each other. It's amazing that she stuck with me while I learned the long process of hanging out with and dating the opposite sex.

This book has given you ideas to help you in your dating experience. You might not be dating now, but eventually you will be. If you've grasped one thing from this book that you'll be able to use when you start dating, then I'm excited!

Before you close this book, though, and get back to dating, read just a few more bits of advice. The following words sum up major portions of the book.

The Rules of Dating

Keep God first.

This might be the toughest rule to follow. But keeping God at the center of your dating relationships is essential. God and his Word are a constant guide for how to treat your date, and for giving you answers to serious dating questions. Spend time alone, praying that God will be honored by your dates, and that he will be glorified in your dating relationships.

Be a friend.

At the heart of every good dating relationship is a strong friendship. Strong friendships help you weather the tough times. A strong friendship is built together over time and through all kinds of experiences. Resist the temptation to build your relationship on shallow attraction and physical sensation.

Be kind.

If you're not interested in someone you're on a first date with, be kind. If you want to break up with the person you've been dating for some time, be kind. If you get dumped and you want to lash out at the other person . . . don't. Be kind. Being kind isn't easy, but it's a necessary part of your dating relationships. *Always* be kind.

Honor your date.

Always do your best to build up the person you're dating. Do what you can to help your date feel the best about himself or herself and about being with you.

Your date is not like you.

You think and feel in a particular way. Your date thinks and feels differently, partly because your date is the opposite sex. Your date is chemically, physically, and mentally different than you. When you date, remember that there are two of you in the relationship. You and your date process information, ideas, and emotions differently.

Go very slowly.

When you begin dating someone you like, your heart can take over, leaving your head in the dust, and leading you to do things that are inappropriate. Some young people often *feel* ready to get married long before they *are really* ready. Take things slowly . . . think before you act. You've got your whole life ahead of you!

Be selective.

Remember one of the famous lines in dating? "There's more fish in the sea!" That statement is true. You don't need to settle for someone you don't fit with, and you don't need to go out with someone who is mean to you. Be careful about the people you date. Make sure you choose to date the people you feel comfortable around and who will treat you like royalty.

Things to Remember Your Entire Dating Life

Ummm . . . your *entire* life? Yeah, I mean that. This book talks about general rules and ideas of dating, but you need to remember some things as you date throughout your life. Remember these things whether you're on your first date, or if you're dating someone seriously, or if you're on your last "official" date before you get married.

A date should not make you feel afraid.

Do you feel fear during your dating experience? Do you feel afraid of your date? Do you feel fear about where your date is taking you? Fear is God's internal guide, his gift to you that helps you know what you should stay away from. If at any time you feel afraid, listen to that emotion and act on it. If you feel afraid, stay away from what's causing the fear.

Dating should not hurt.

You feel pain for a reason. If you stick a pin in your arm, your body responds with pain to a foreign object. Dating is the same way. If you're experiencing pain in a dating relationship, it's probably because something unnatural is happening.

Dating should not cause you to sin.

Duh! But really, no relationship should cause you to step away from God and do something that's against his desire and plan for you. When a relationship causes you to commit an act against God's laws, that relationship is sinful. How do you know what's sinful? First, if you know God's word, you'll know what sin is. Second, if you're a believer, God's Holy Spirit will guide you into knowing what is right and wrong. You'll know you're sinning if you feel nervous or guilty about what you're doing.

Dating should be an awesome experience.

When you go out with someone, you ought to have a great time. Any experience with someone you like—the movies or dinner or wherever—ought to be great. Dating can and should be an experience that you remember forever. Have fun. You deserve it.

Every relationship, including your dates, ought to help you become God's person.

Dating should bring out the best in you.

Remember—God has created you to be a particular kind of person. He created no one else like you. You are not a copy of someone else. You are not a mistake. God's plan for you includes meeting people who will bring out the person he wants you to be. *Every* relationship, including your dates, ought to help you become God's person. Every relationship, including your dates, should bring out the best in you.

Your dating life should honor God, and it should honor you. That is my prayer for you. Any person you date should be committed to living their life fully for God. Any person you date should have a desire to help you be the person God wants you to be.

Dating is awesome when it glorifies God. May he bless you as you leap into the world of dating.

⇒ Connecting with Yourself

- Write down one thing that freaks you out about dating. Tape it to your bathroom mirror, and pray about it each day.

⇒ Connecting with Your Friends

- Get together with one friend and make a list of the positive things that can happen in your dating life. As you continue to date, remember the positives about dating.

→ ## Connecting with Your Parents

- Ask your parents to pray for you as you attempt to glorify God with your dating life. Ask them to be willing to guide you and give you advice about dating throughout your adolescence.

→ ## Connecting with God

- Ask God to help you become an awesome person to date. Ask him to give you self-confidence, a focus on him, and the endurance to be his child while you date others. Commit to praying daily and asking God to be the center of your dating life. Ask him to help you glorify him with each date.

Fourteen

Date Ideas

Deciding what to do on a date isn't always easy. After you work up the nerve to ask someone out for a first date, or make time in your schedule for a date with someone you're already committed to, you need to think of someplace to go. Should you go out for dinner? What about just taking a walk?

Whether you're stumped for an idea for a first date or need a new idea to spark up a current relationship, this list will help.

Friend Dates and First Dates

1. Ice Cream

Don't underestimate even the simplest of dates. Going out for ice cream is the easiest, least expensive date you can go on and still spend money. Don't let this remain a simple date, though. Talk to your date. Use the time together to ask your date questions about himself or herself. What was your date like when he or she was little? What does your date want to do for a career?

2. A Park

Push each other on the swings. See who can go down the slides the fastest. Play in the dirt. Going to the park is the old standard in dating practices. It's an oldie, and a goodie, too.

3. A Zoo

The zoo is a cool place to get a conversation going with someone you're still getting comfortable around. Try to find animals that look like your family members. Talk about the kinds of food the animals eat.

4. The Movies

Going to a movie together is a great way to hang out in a non-threatening situation. But don't allow the movie to kill your opportunities for talking. Try going to a movie that isn't crowded, and where you won't interrupt people if you whisper. During the movie, ask your date questions about what's happening on the screen.

5. Rent a Movie

Renting a movie and going to one of your houses is another non-threatening way to get to know each other. As you watch the movie, don't just clam up—talk about what's happening in the plot or about the characters. At this early stage in dating, rent a comedy. It'll get you two talking and laughing together.

6. A Christian Concert

Concerts aren't the best place to get to know your date, but they're a great place to have a shared experience. Pick a concert that you and your date's parents agree features music that's okay to listen to. Go, have a great time, and chalk up the evening together as an opportunity to get comfortable with each other.

7. Watch a Favorite TV Show

This is like watching a movie together, but you've got more to talk about. Tell the other person why the show is your favorite. Talk about what you're watching.

8. Watch a Sunset

Sitting and watching the sky isn't as boring—or as romantic—as you might think. If you're sitting together and concentrating on the horizon, you're most likely talking and sharing information about yourselves. Spending time watching a sunset means that you're enjoying and learning more about each other.

9. Play a Sport

No fair playing a sport that one of you plays better than the other. Pick a sport at which neither of you are experts, and play it together. If your date is an expert at all sports, level the odds by giving both of you a handicap—like each tying one hand behind his or her back, or playing blindfolded.

10. A Sports Game

Watching a game and talking about what's happening is a good way to get to know each other. Here's a twist—go to a game where neither of you know anyone who's playing. Pick a team and cheer for it. Eat some of the food that's sold at the game.

11. Yard Work

Want to know your date's tolerance for work? Like to know how much work your date can handle? Choose one of your homes and do the yard work together. This is a great date, and it helps the two of you see each other in less than desirable circumstances.

12. Go Fishing

Fishing isn't just about fishing. It's about hanging out, learning about patience, and getting to know the person you're fishing with. Find a place where you and your date can fish alone. While you're waiting to catch a fish, talk about whatever comes to mind.

13. Plant Stuff

Planting things together is another way to spend time with your date and get to know that person. This activity helps the two of you share an experience, get dirty together, and give an area some new growth.

14. Watch the News

Watching the news can get you and your date talking about current events. Ask your date what he or she thinks about what's happening in the world, and tell what you think about it.

15. Do Homework

You can find out a lot about someone when you study with that person. Get your books, choose a place (either your house or the other person's), and do your homework together. Be sure to take study breaks!

16. Fly a Kite

Not many things are more challenging than flying a kite. Get a cheap kite, find an open field, and try to get the thing to fly. Take turns running and holding the kite. When you finally launch it and it stays in the air, help each other make the kite do tricks by yanking on the string.

17. Ride Horses

This one may not be so easy to arrange. You've got to have a friend who will let you ride his or her horses, or know of a stable close by that rents horses. Riding horses gives the two of you an opportunity to experience something unusual together. Shared unusual experiences help create a bond with the person you're dating. And, for some of us, riding horses is definitely an unusual experience.

18. Walk a Dog

There's something about hanging out with an animal that can get two people talking. Find a dog (yours, your date's, or a neighbor's) and invite your date out for a walk. As you're walking the dog, talk about the kinds of pets you've owned in your life. Talk about the kinds of pets you want to own when you're older.

19. Bowling

No one looks comfortable or elegant while bowling. That makes bowling a perfect sport for you and your date. Even if you don't know the correct way to score a bowling game . . . go, wear the silly shoes, and have a great time.

20. Skating

Roller-skating gives the two of you time to talk about anything. Go to a roller rink, skate along to the music, and eat food at the concession stand. If you don't have a rink in your town, roller blade through a park or in your neighborhood. It's a fun thing to do together that doesn't involve eating or watching movies.

21. Yard Sales

Sifting through someone else's junk can help you learn a lot about each other. Spend a Saturday morning going to several yard sales. Notice what stuff your date likes and what level of "worn out" is acceptable to him or her.

22. Bike Ride

Riding bikes is an alternative to going for a walk, and it gives you a chance to talk. We're not talking about a marathon ride—you don't need to race each other. Pick a park or a road that's less traveled, ride and talk.

23. Paint a Picture

Anytime you can create something with a person, you're learning about how that person views life and how artistic he or she is. Painting a picture with your date, then, is a great way to learn more about him or her. Together, get some paints and either a canvas or a sheet of paper. Choose a subject (either a bowl of fruit or something outside) and paint the picture together. If you're more daring, get two sets of paint, two sheets of paper, and paint a portrait of each other. When you're done, show each other what you've painted.

24. Clean a Room

Want to know how your date cleans? Interested in how fast he or she works? This one will help you. Spend time cleaning a room in either your house or your date's. As you clean, talk about the messes in your life and the things that clutter your house.

25. Go for a Walk

A simple walk together can help you and your date get to know each other. But this isn't a walk for exercise; it's a walk for enjoyment. Walk and talk—get to know each other.

26. Amusement Park

Spend a day riding roller coasters and eating amusement park food.

27. Clean Out a Garage

Give your time to someone in your church or to one of your own garages. Work together to clean, straighten, and organize the garage.

28. Pet Store

Pet stores are good places to get in touch with your date's feelings. Go to a pet store and hold as many of the animals as the owners will allow. Notice the animals that your date likes most, and talk about the kinds of animals that are your favorites.

29. Window Shopping

Not shopping for a new window . . . walk a mall and don't go inside any of the stores. Look at the displays in the windows, and talk about the kinds of things you might buy if you had a million dollars.

30. Random Acts of Kindness

Spend a day looking for fun and creative ways to serve others. Buy a candy bar at a grocery store and then give it to the cashier. Wash someone's car windshield at a gas station. See how many doors you can open for people in one night. It's a great way to have fun together and show God's love to others.

31. Library or Bookstore

Find out what interests your date by finding out what he or she likes to read. Many large bookstores have cafés where you can just sit and talk, and fun children's sections where you could read some of your favorite childhood books to each other.

32. Try Foreign Foods

Get adventurous and try something new together by going to a restaurant serving Middle Eastern, Thai, Ethiopian, or other types of unfamiliar foods. It may be delicious or just plain frightening, but no matter what, it will give you something to talk about!

33. Play a Board Game

It's a rainy day favorite. Board games are great because they're fun to play and they don't take so much of your attention that you can't talk.

Dates for Serious Daters

1. Take a Personality Inventory

If you know someone who is licensed to give personality tests, have him or her test you and the person you're dating. Then have the tester separately walk each of you through the results. When you're finished, share the results that you're comfortable with sharing, and talk about those areas where you're compatible as well as areas where you need a little work.

2. Go on a Date with Your Parents

Going on a date with your parents is a great way to learn even more about your date. Your parents have a lot of information about dating they could share with you. As you double-date with them, ask for their advice about dating, and pick up some pointers by observing them.

3. Eat Dinner at Your Date's House

It's not usually easy to get to know your date's family. If you don't already know them, you might feel awkward around them. So invite yourself over to their house for a meal that the whole family will be sitting down to. As you're eating, ask the family to tell funny stories about your date when he or she was younger.

4. Cook Dinner

An alternative to just eating at your date's house is to actually cook the meal together. Cooking is a great way to learn about each others habits, and watching how someone cooks can tell you how that person thinks. As you cook, talk about your favorite foods and what kinds of things you eat most often.

5. Go on a Date with a Mentor Couple

Invite a couple that you respect from your church to go on a date with you and your date. Go someplace where the four of you can talk. Ask them if they have any dating tips that might help you and your date have a happier, healthier dating relationship.

6. Play Monopoly

If you'd like to know how your date handles money or how ruthless that person is, play Monopoly together. Monopoly can take a long time to play, so expect to be involved with this for a while. As you play, talk about finances and your date's financial expectations for his or her career.

7. A Romantic Dinner

Nothing beats a dinner out. Pick a place that's romantic, where the staff really takes care of you. Try choosing food for each other.

8. Eat Lunch in a Park

Have you ever noticed how eating with someone can be sort of intimate? You can get to know a lot about someone when you eat with that person. So put together a picnic lunch and eat it together in a park.

9. Attend a Ceramics Workshop

Sign up for a ceramics class and create something together. If the instructor allows, create something that represents how each of you feels about the other person. When the project is done, share ownership of the creation, each of you keeping it for a month at a time.

10. Art Gallery

Looking at art can be an effective way to learn about your date's thoughts and feelings. Go to an art gallery. It doesn't have to be a full-fledged museum. Any art gallery will do. Slowly, walk through and talk about which works you like most, and how your favorites make you feel.

11. Volunteer for Community Service

Loads of places in your community are probably looking for people to volunteer some time. Consider volunteering with your date at a children's home, picking up trash along a creek, doing repair projects for senior citizens.

12. Volunteer to Work in Your Church Nursery

Your church could probably use some help in their nursery. Working together in a nursery, you and your date can observe how each of you handles small children and deals with stress.

13. An Opera, Ballet, or Symphony

Like going to an art gallery, going to a symphony or ballet can help you and your date learn each other's thoughts and feelings on an artistic level. Pick a performance that you both agree on, and one that you can afford.

14. Talk with Your Date's Grandparents

Your date's grandparents have a huge amount of information about your date. Together, visit your date's grandparents and ask them what your date was like when he or she was younger.

15. Retirement Home

Serving others with your date is an excellent activity for learning more about each other and to help you grow closer. Call ahead and ask if there's anything you can do to help out at the home, then go and serve together.

16. Drive

Going for a drive and talking about life can be an excellent way to learn more about the person you're dating. Drive, and talk about any topic that comes to mind. Use this opportunity to learn how to listen to what your date says.

17. Learn to Do Work on a Car

Have one of your parents—or someone who knows something about mechanics—teach the two of you the basics of car maintenance. Ask the one teaching to go slowly, and make sure that you both understand how to do what's being taught.

18. Homeless Shelter

Serving together is a great way to learn about what your date values and how he or she deals with very different circumstances. Call ahead and plan to serve a meal at a homeless shelter. While you're serving at the shelter, talk with the homeless people.

19. Look at Baby Pictures

You and your date each gather a stack of your baby pictures and then trade. Spend time looking at each other's baby pictures and talking about your childhoods.

20. Interview Your Parents

Life has changed since your parents were your age. Ask your parents to sit down and talk about what they were like when they were your age.

21. Look at Each Other

You've seen your date—but have you *seen* that person? Do you know all of the lines and dots on his or her face? Do you know the shape of that person's mouth when he or she smiles? Find a quiet place and look at each other. Don't talk, don't crack jokes, and don't make silly faces. Just look at each other.

22. Go Clothes Shopping

Want to know exactly what kind of clothes your date likes? Need ideas for what to buy your date for his or her birthday? Go clothes shopping. Pay attention to the styles your date likes. For fun, each of you pick an outfit that you think would look great on the other person.

23. Movie Idea—Rent a Romance

Watching a romance is different than watching a comedy. Rent a romance, and talk about the relationship of the people in the movie. Do you like the way they treat each other? How would you feel if you lived like the people in the movie?

24. Send an Encouraging E-mail to Missionaries

The Internet makes sending encouraging notes to missionaries very easy. Choose one missionary that each of you knows, get together, and write an encouraging e-mail to that person.

25. Take Your Youth Pastor Out for Lunch

Your youth pastor would love to have someone buy him or her a free meal. Invite that person out, and then ask him or her to give you relationship tips. Also, have your youth pastor tell you his or her dating history.

26. Video Letters

Spend one week videotaping your inner feelings about each other. Do this in the privacy of your home when you're not with the other person. At the end of the week show each other your videotapes.

27. Do a Word Study

Pick a word like *love* and research the meaning of the word in Scripture. Look up the word in Bible dictionaries, concordances, Greek dictionaries, etc. When you've studied the word and its meanings, ask yourselves how your love for each other reflects God's love.

28. Take a Day Trip

Loads of interesting places are probably near where you live, places that you've never really seen. Look around in the area near your hometown for things you've always wanted to check out. When you've found a place, invite another couple to go with you, and spend the day exploring a new place.

29. Look at Clouds

You've probably spent time outside with your date, but have you ever noticed the sky? Looking at clouds is really more than just looking at clouds. When you look at clouds, talk about what you see or how you feel. Looking at clouds and talking about them might help you open up about something the two of you have never talked about.

30. Read the Book of Ecclesiastes

The book of Ecclesiastes makes a lot of thought provoking statements. Take turns reading the book aloud. When you're done reading, talk about how the thoughts in the book might apply to or relate to your life.

31. Spend One Day Apart

This might sound like a crazy kind of date, but try not spending any time together. While you're apart, try not to think about the other person. When you get back together, you'll probably enjoy each other more and you'll possibly have a lot to talk about.